Towards a Diasporic Imagination of the Present: an eternal

sense of Homelessness

Towards a Diasporic Imagination of the Present: an eternal sense of Homelessness.

Anne Murphy, Rina Williams and Sean O Dubhghaill.

Edited by: Tapati Bharadwaj.

Published by

LIES AND BIG FEET

ISBN: 9384281050

ISBN-13: 978-9384281052

CONTENTS

LIST OF CONTRIBUTORS

RINA VERMA WILLIAMS is Assistant Professor of Political Science at the University of Cincinnati, where she is also Affiliate Faculty in Asian Studies and Women's, Gender and Sexuality Studies. Her research and teaching interests focus on comparative Indian politics, religion and nationalism, and gender and identity politics. She is the author of *Postcolonial Politics and Personal Laws: Colonial Legal Legacies and the Indian State* (Oxford University Press) as well as several articles, book chapters and book reviews. Her current book project examines the role of women in religious nationalism in Indian democracy and political parties.

A(t) Home in the World: Refiguring (Indian) National Identity in a Global Era

The concept of diaspora contains embedded within itself the concept of a national home—and thus, a national identity. Much ink has been spilled by scholars asking whether, or how, globalization spells the end of national identity. In an era of unceasing circulation and flow of people, capital, cultures and identities across national borders, it seems facile and easy to assume that national identity must inevitably wither away. In this essay I argue that rather than withering away in an era of neoliberal globalization, national identity instead has reconfigured, reinvented and adapted itself to be "at home in the world." To demonstrate this I focus on Indian national identity, tracing its permutations since the 1980s through three interwoven narratives: my own personal experiences as a scholar of Indian origin who grew up in the United States; the political liberalization of the Indian state and economy; and the shifting portrayals of Indians, the west, and Indian national identity in popular Bollywood cinema. Through these lenses, I argue that where Indian national identity itself was more closed

i

and insular prior to the 1980s, Since then Indian national identity has expanded into the world—globalizing itself—in such a way as to make itself globally present while retaining the core essence of a national identity that constructs itself as innately unique even as it demonstrates its ability to stand on its own in the global arena. This suggests the possibility of the neo-liberalization of national identity itself: unmoored, no longer anchored to governments or even geographic terrains, national identity itself becomes diasporic, joining the very unceasing flows and circulations of the globalization that we once feared might destroy it.

ANNE MURPY (Ph.D. Columbia) is Associate Professor in the Department of Asian Studies at the University of British Columbia. She teaches and conducts research on the cultural and religious history of Punjab. Her monograph, *The Materiality of the Past: History and Representation in Sikh Tradition* (Oxford University Press, 2012), explores the construction of Sikh memory and historical consciousness in texts, objects and sites from the eighteenth century to the twentieth. Current research concerns the Punjabi language movement and modern Punjabi literature in the Indian and Pakistani Punjabs and in the Punjabi speaking Diaspora.

A Diasporic Temporality: New narrative writing from Punjabi-Canada

This paper describes an emergent ethos of the diasporic subject in narrative fiction from the Punjabi-Canadian diaspora of British Columbia in relation to the past and around the central idea and experience of translation. This ethos is discerned primarily through the expression of time and the experience of memory. In this I follow on Brian Axel's (2002) suggestion a decade ago that we dis-place the centrality of "location" in our analytical construction of the diaspora. Instead he argues that, alongside corporeality and affect, temporality must be configured centrally in our understanding of the workings of a "diasporic imaginary" that produces diasporic subjects. Our focus is *Vigocā*, by Jarnail Singh Sekha (2011), within the context of other works written by Punjabi Canadian authors. We will pay particular attention to its treatment of the past, as both a continuing presence in our present and as a way of marking subjectivity in in relation to that-which-is-lost, a sensibility of both loss and gain, presence and absence. Indeed, that is the meaning of the term "Vigoca"--loss or lack. This term also encapsulates the theme of translation, writ as both cultural and linguistic, written in Punjabi and describing the hegemony of English within it. Temporality and language interact in dynamic ways with multiple forms of place-making, both in adherence to the "fragile—yet enduring—ground of the nation form," as Axel notes, but also exceeding and complicating that form through the temporal and locative displacements that are possible in the fictive world (2002, 426). The articulation of personal and community history in the work suggests new ways of thinking about the diasporic subject as a temporal aspect, produced perhaps as an effect within a linguistic interface, and how these forces impinge on the present-making project.

SEAN O DUBHGHAILL is an Anthropologist currently working for the Interculturalism, Migrations and Minorities Research Centre at KU Leuven. He is currently working to complete his Ph.D in Cultural Anthropology on the Irish Diaspora in Europe. His academic interests concern the Anthropological Epistemology, Representation and Minority Languages.

Imagining the Present and (re)presenting the Imaginary: Belonging and 'homelessness' among the Irish Diaspora in Belgium

The recent turn in the social sciences, which emphasises the role played by the social and cultural imaginary (Taylor, 2004; Salazar and Graburn, 2013), presents an interesting lens through which the concept of diaspora can be (re)imagined. Taking the imaginary as our jumping off point we can ask long-standing questions anew; imaginaries, therefore, can help us inform the manner through which Diasporic groups imagine 'home', mobilities, sameness and otherness, the past as well as their possible future(s).

If we adhere to Anderson's (1983) maxim that communities are imagined entities, diasporic communities are in a sense doubly-imagined, given that they are not at home, but a sense of commonality still remains. How sameness and difference are imagined among the diaspora seems to depend largely upon the extent of engagement with the host country. Examining the Irish in Belgium is an excellent case study to this end, given the language barriers as well as the interrelated history the two countries share. The shared history informs the diaspora's imaginary in two ways, both the older history which extends back as far as 1607, when Franciscan migrants were housed in Belgium's historic University in Louvain, as well as more recent history when Ireland joined the European Union, whose major institutions are in Brussels, in 1973.

This work examines how members of the Irish diaspora (thought to be 80 million-strong worldwide) recapitulate a sense of belonging in Belgium by reproducing or simulating products of national belonging and identity (music, sports and social life in particular). How the Irish diaspora are imagined to make a home in Belgium, and thereby to stave off the negative effects of isolation, 'homelessness' and anomie, is the central objective of this prospective work.

〰〰〰〰〰〰〰〰〰〰〰〰〰〰〰〰〰〰〰〰〰〰〰〰〰〰〰〰〰

INTRODUCTION

TAPATI BHARADWAJ

This collection of three essays looks at the notion of diasporic identity. It is not redundant to ask if we, who are situated in the present, are more conscious and self-reflexive about our dislocated situatedness? Michael North describes the sense of restlessness which defines global travel as a modern phenomenon; where the desire to travel is so "relentless that citizenship ceases to have any meaning, as does the difference between home and abroad"[1] It would be rather simplistic to argue that people are traveling or migrating (for socio-political-economic reasons) more frequently than usual in the early 21st century but there does seem to be a heightened sense of reflexivity about the Self-Other/ home-foreign dichotomy which compels and allows the migrant traveler to document and

---

[1] Michael North, *Reading 1922: A Return to the Scene of the Modern* (New York: Oxford University Press, 1999), p. 12.

reflect about the socio-psychical processes that accompany this displacement. The movement from place A to place B, as a result of socio-cultural-economic imperatives, creates an awareness of the differences between both the places, making one conclude that there must be a desire within us which allows us to recognize difference and negotiate with it. These three essays examine this notion of displacement and the emergence of multiple realms of cultures which coexist alongside the dominant ones.

A genealogy of recorded diasporic identity in the last two centuries.

But not all diasporic identities are necessarily pleasure ridden; some have emerged as a result of socio-political affiliations, which often accompany disenfranchisement. The African-American identity, in the early twentieth century, was one that was under constant fluidity. If we consider a journal like *The Crisis*, which was edited by William Du Bois, we can get a clearer understanding of the global nature of the African American identity that emerged in the early 20th century. As the editor of *The Crisis*, William Du Bois could "sway vast segments of Afro-American opinion."[2] The Crisis was read by a large audience than the middle class intelligentsia and in an age of "rampant illiteracy … the magazine found its way into kerosene-lit sharecroppers' cabins and cramped factory tenements."[3] Du Bois articulated a sense of global black belonging, that was also specifically American; an identity, as

---

[2] David Levering Lewis, *When Harlem was in Vogue* (New York: Knopf, 1981), p. 6.

[3] Ibid., 7.

Alys Weinbaum writes, that argues for "African-American inclusion in the nation" and also for "black belonging to the world."[4]

The diasporic condition, of being slaves and immigrants in the western world, is a psychical by-product of various geo-political conditions. Jacqueline Mc Leod writes about the "international dimensions" in the histories and narratives of the black diasporic community[5] and what they share, she argues, is a common set of experiences of slavery and racism and socio-economic disenfranchisement. On a similar note, Stuart Hall writes that diaspora "does not refer to those scattered tribes whose identity can only be secured in relationship to some sacred homeland to which they must at all cost return, even if it means pushing other people into the sea"[6] and infact, diaspora identities "are those which are constantly producing and reproducing themselves anew, through transformation and difference."[7] What is not surprising is that there also exists a large body of writings by African Americans from the early 1800s which talks about such concepts of diasporic citizenship.

Written in 1830 in antebellum America, David Walker's "Our Wretchedness in Consequence of the Colonizing Plan"[8]

---

[4] Alys Weinbaum, "Reproducing Racial Globality: W. E. B. DuBois and the Sexual Politics of Black Nationalism" *Social Text* 67 # 19: 2, Summer 2001, pp15-41, 15-16.

[5] Jacqueline Mc Leod, *Crossing Boundaries: Comparative History of Black People in Diaspora* (Bloomington: Indiana University Press, 1999).

[6] Stuart Hall, "Cultural identity and diaspora." in *Identity: Community, Culture, Difference*, Ed. J. Rutherford (London: Lawrence and Wishart, 1990), pp. 222-37, p. 235.

[7] Ibid., p. 235.

[8] David Walker, "Our Wretchedness in Consequence of the Colonizing Plan" in *David Walker's Appeal to the Coloured Citizens of the World*, ed. Peter P. Hinks

refuses to allow the African American to simply belong to
Africa; this text is an outright rejection of the plans of the
American Colonization Society, which was formed in 1817 to
enable the emigration of free African-Americans to Liberia, and
reveals a refusal to establish a pure African identity. It is not
possible to arrive at a reductive notion of racial solidarity and
we cannot make an easy equation between the African-
American and the African and for Walker, the African-
American is always caught between multiple identities. Walker
also refers to the English as the African American's greatest
friends, and simultaneously aligns himself with Haiti where a
revolution against the French had taken place in 1791 (and
ended in 1803).[9] For a disenfranchised African American of the
antebellum period, the processes of belonging were never
stable, as Walker makes clear and cannot be limited to either the
United States or to Africa, but have to be seen as being in a
state of constant disjuncture, where the diasporic imagination
exists in un-home like spaces. Even before the Colonization
Society voiced plans of re-settling free blacks into Liberia, a
similar concern had been expressed by a group of "Free
Africans" led by Prince Hall who wrote a petition to the
General Court of Massachusetts in 1787 with a plan to resettle
in Africa, due to their "disagreeable and disadvantageous
circumstances" in the United States; in Africa they would be
living among equals. The emergence of a disaporic
consciousness was a result of certain socio-legal conditions that
the African Americans faced in the United States, and also
reveals a heightened sense of self reflexivity.

(University Park: Penn State Press, 2000), pp. 47-82.

[9] Ibid., p. 58.

A similar argument is made by Paul Gilroy in *The Black Atlantic*, where he draws attention to the formation of black diasporic communities across the Atlantic in the nineteenth century that created a transnational black identity.[10] Gilroy argues against 'insiderism' which uses national ethnic fixity and instead, proposes for fluid identities. Gilroy writes that the Black Atlantic can be defined "through [a] desire to transcend both the structures of the nation state and the constraints of ethnicity and national particularity."[11] And this is clearly evident in the writings of David Walker, where we see a desire to transcend the boundary of any one single national identity, and a simultaneous disclaimer that he be not limited to a transatlantic space of the United States and Africa, for Walker transgressively conjures up Haiti and England as possible homes; for the African American, identity was in a state of constant disarray. [12] Such diasporic spaces exist at the interstices of national-ethnic identity, citizenship and racial affiliations.

The presence of the diasporic imagination need not necessarily be specific to the experiences of the black American, as the antebellum period in America saw a large number of European immigrants entering the United States who were integrated within the United States and given full citizenship

---

[10] Paul Gilroy, *The Black Atlantic: Modernity and Double Consciousness* (London: Verso, 1993).

[11] Ibid., p. 19.

[12] This is an underlying note in David Walker's writings: "Is there not land in America, or 'corn enough in Egypt?' Why should they send us into a far country to die? See the thousands of foreigners emigrating to America every year: and if there be ground sufficient for them to cultivate, and bread for them to eat, why would they wish to send the first *tillers* of the land away? ... this land which we have watered with our *tears* and our *blood*, is now our *mother country*, and we are well satisfied to stay." p. 60.

rights, but retained desires and memories of the past. Matthew Jacobson argues that the identity of these new immigrant communities (referring to the Polish, Jewish and Irish communities) was intertwined within a "diasporic imagination" which he defines as that "sense of undying membership in, and unyielding obligation to, a distant national community."[13] Despite their cultural allegiance to a distant land, all whites were granted citizenship in the Naturalization Law of 1789.[14] The privilege of whiteness was not automatically conferred onto whites, but violently struggled for; the new immigrants – Teutons, Slav, Hebrew, Celt, Alpine – were never positioned in a homogeneous identity of whiteness and instead, what emerges is how contradictory "racial identities [came] to coexist at the same moment in the same body in unstable combinations."[15] Citizenship, in this particular instance, was never contained within a single cultural parameter and in fact, embraced numerous identities.

Imperial Diasporic citizenry in colonial India.

Within a completely different socio-historical context of British

---

[13] Matthew Jacobson, *Special Sorrows: The Diasporic Imagination of Irish, Polish, and Jewish Immigrants in the United States* (Berkeley: University of California Press, 2002), p. 10.

[14] Dispelling the myth that America was founded on racial inclusion, Jacobson proposes that whiteness and its privileges had been "among the central organizers of the political life of the republic" drawing attention to how "national subjectivity" and "national belonging" were both "inflected by racial conception of peoplehood, self possession, firmness for self government and collective destiny." p. 21.

[15] Jacobson, *Whiteness of a Different Color: European Immigrants and the Alchemy of Race* (Cambridge: Harvard University Press, 1999), p. 142.

colonization in India, we see the emergence of imperial-diasporic citizenry. The process of creating a new identity of imperial-diasporic citizens in the late eighteenth century in colonial India happened as a result of the geographical translocation that accompanied colonization. For the British citizen in colonial India, imperial-diasporic citizenship was made possible through the consumption of not only texts that made their way across continents from England to the colonies, but also through the establishment of the different socio-cultural realms within the newly established colonial city of Calcutta. The newly established realm of print and newspapers formed a large part of the texts that were consumed, and aided in establishing and perpetuating a notion of imperial diasporic citizenship.

This early realm of print played an important role in allowing those in the colonies to imagine themselves as always connected with the metropole, thus establishing and maintaining a sense of diasporic citizenship within the imagination of the readers. For an English reader, situated in Bengal, it would have been meaningful for him to be reading news about England, and global affairs, despite being disconnected socially and culturally from his immediate surroundings in Calcutta. Even though he was reading news about wars being fought on the continent and social events of the royal family that were six months old (the time it took for a ship to sail from Britain to India), it allowed the reader to participate in the public functioning of the Empire. Print technology, thus, enabled the far flung colonies to be brought under the umbrella of empire building, paving the way for a notion of diasporic citizenship to be cultivated. A proper system of printing newspapers was established, and so was a postal order which distributed these newspapers in the districts.[16]

There is a correlation between the fact that this realm of print culture, that was imported to India by the English and was an aid in establishing and perpetuating a sense of diasporic citizenship, occurred at a time period when there was a movement of people across the globe who also used print to articulate their desires to be citizens of multiple worlds. It is not a stretch of the imagination to argue that such notions of being imperial citizens – despite being away from the center of power in England – has to be seen as part of this phenomenon of diasporic citizenship being articulated by other communities in this time period, and reflects a sense of self reflexivity.

Conclusion: normalizing perpetual travel.

Would it be too irrational for us to state that we are, at the moment, currently poised to do away with simple assumptions which equate citizenship as being contained within monolithic identities. With the constant flow of people all across the world, we have become self-reflexive enough to theorize about this; more importantly, we project these anxieties and reflections onto the public realm, allowing ourselves agency to re-conceptualize fundamental notions of culture, identity and citizenship.

---

[16] For more, see Mrinal Kanti Chanda, *The History of the English Press in* Bengal (Calcutta: K.P. Bagchi, 1988), pp. 452-465.

THE PLAY OF TIME AND LANGUAGE: CANADIAN FICTION IN PUNJABI

ANNE MURPHY

The Punjabi language literary environment of British Columbia is vibrant, and works written here express both interests in South Asia (particularly in India) and local concerns. This essay addresses in preliminary terms—as a part of a larger project—the temporality imbedded within diasporic literary production and its relationship with language in recent narrative fiction from the Punjabi-Canadian diaspora of British Columbia, Canada. In pursuing this I follow on Brian Axel's suggestion a decade ago that we dis-place the centrality of "location" in our analytical construction of the diaspora. He argues instead that temporality, alongside corporeality and affect, must be configured centrally in our understanding of the workings of a "diasporic imaginary" that produces diasporic subjects, where the image of a whole and complete past allows for the present but is not necessarily the location of a nostalgic return.[1] Axel locates such a temporal movement among images of Sikh bodies marked by violence that proliferate on the internet, but a similar kind of temporality holds perhaps even more so in the fictive world of representation in the novel and short story. As I will show, this temporal aspect interacts in dynamic ways with multiple forms of place-making, as well as language, both in adherence to the "fragile—yet enduring—ground of the nation form," as Axel notes, but also exceeding and complicating that form through its temporal aspect and the locative and linguistic displacements that are possible in the fictive world.[2] It also must be located in the specific intersections that shape Punjabi literature as a transnational phenomenon.

My focus is works of narrative fiction written in Punjabi by authors based in Canada, to explore their temporal, spacial, and linguistic dimensions, and particularly their sense of the continuing presence of the past and sensibility of both loss and gain, presence and absence--and how this is configured in relation to the experience of language. The ways personhood and community are formed in the works examined here suggest the profitability of thinking about the diasporic as a temporal rather than locative logic, and how the past impinges on and simultaneously enables the present-making project articulated in complex ways through language. At the same time that I focus on temporality and language, however, I must note the dynamic nature of place-making in the work of the Punjabi-speaking Diaspora of greater Vancouver. This is perhaps most vividly demonstrated in Vancouver in the renaming that occurs with

---

[1] Brian Keith Axel "The Diasporic Imaginary" in *Public Culture* 14, 2 (2002): 411-428, see pg. 412, 424, 426.

[2] Axel, "The Diasporic Imaginary," 426.

reference to the journal *"Watanoṅ Dūr"*—"far from the homeland"—which was founded in 1973 in greater Vancouver and published until 1986. After the journal closed, it was revived under a new name: *Watan*, or "homeland," which continued until 1995, and then was brought to life again in 2007 as an online magazine.[3] The homeland came home to Canada, and was fully enabled to do so by the internet.

Why Punjabi literature?

Writing in Punjabi is by its very nature a politically and socially marked act. This is so in literary terms, as well as conventional political ones. Indeed, to write in any Indian vernacular is to fight a transnational battle. Salman Rushdie's now famous 1997 dismissal of writing in South Asian vernaculars asserted a cultural ascendancy for Indian writing in English, such that fiction and nonfiction produced "by Indian writers working in English is proving to be a stronger and more important body of work than most of what has been produced in the eighteen 'recognized' languages of India."[4] V.S. Naipaul asserted a similar sentiment at a 2002 conference in Delhi. While such a position clearly disregards vernacular writing out of sheer ignorance, the global politics of English and the economics of the publishing industry ensure the persistence of a divide between English literary zones and those of vernacular literatures. Yet, as I'll show, the work of diasporic writers in Punjabi (as may be true for work in other languages) challenges the basic formulations that feed conventional divisions between linguistic realms, and among diaspora literatures.

---

[3] See history at: http://watanarchives.wordpress.com

[4] Iyer and Zare *Other Tongues*, xix.

Rushdie and others' statements about vernacular literature rely upon certain assumptions: South Asian writing in English internationally as well as in South Asia is seen to reflect an inherently transnational orientation, reflecting its authors' identities-in-motion and the material conditions of their lives. (This is the diaspora fiction, that written in English, that has received so much attention to date.) Such a simple characterization is problematic, even without considering the nature of writing in languages other than English; it is even more so when we do. South Asian writing in vernacular languages, such as Punjabi, is conventionally said to concern itself with the local texture of life, and possess less with a global reach. While certainly such characterizations to a degree do hold—the preoccupation of many modern writers in South Asia from Premchand to Ismat Chughtai was indeed to explore the particular and the local, as has indeed been the concern of modern writers all over the world—it is also clearly the case that such an absolute distinction in orientation doesn't hold. When one considers the work of Kartar Singh Duggal, Zubair Ahmed, or Ajeet Kaur, for example, one sees vivid examples of how locally articulated stories function in very global terms, the "singularly plural" that Anita Anantharam describes in her study of modern Hindi and Urdu poetry by women.[5] S. Shankar has suggested the idea of "vernacular postcolonialism," with its "focus on the rooted, the culturally autonomous, and the local" as a way to distinguish vernacular orientations from the "transnational with its focus on the diasporic, the hybrid, the global" which generalizes English-language writing, as a way to valorize the "complicated and varied forms' of the literature of

---

[5] Anita Anantharam. *Bodies that Remember: Women's Indigenous Knowledge and Cosmopolitanism in South Asian Poetry* (Syracuse: Syracuse University Press, 2012), 15.

the vernacular.[6] This is a useful way to reformulate the dialectic between these two literary and linguistic orientations, and resonates with a larger discourse on the need to complicate and inflect the idea of the cosmopolitan, visible in attempts by scholars like Sugata Bose, for example, to assert universalisms ("universalism with a difference") located in vernacular contexts. His concept of a colorful cosmopolitanism seeks to replace the generic and universalist "colorless cosmopolitanism" of Martha Nussbaum and others with a locally defined but no less universalist embrace of the world—akin to the "vernacular cosmopolitanism" of Homi Bhabha, and "rooted cosmopolitanism" of Anthony Appiah.[7]

Recent work by Farina Mir has revealed the history of what she calls a "Punjabi literary formation" in nineteenth and early twentieth century Punjab, formed outside of direct colonial control and expressive of a local and yet cosmopolitan vision of being Punjabi.[8] This cosmopolitan vision, steeped in a non-religiously inflected sense of *punjabiyat* or "Punjabiness", is one that ran counter to the more divisive religiously defined political identities also found in colonial Punjab—and which figured in the partition of the province between Pakistan and India in 1947. Tariq Rahman has noted that one of the earliest datable uses we have for Punjabi from a text in the 1620s is as "the means to an educational end," to learn Persian[9]; it was neither

---

[6] Iyer and Zare *Other Tongues*, 163.

[7] Sugata Bose "Different universalisms, colorful cosmopolitanisms: the global imagination of the colonized" in *Cosmopolitan Thought Zones: South Asia and the Global Circulation of Ideas*, 97-111, edited by Sugata Bose and Kris Manjapra, (NY: Palgrave Macmillan,2010), 97-8.

[8] Farina Mir *The Social Space of Language: Vernacular Culture in British Colonial Punjab* (Berkeley: University of California Press, 2010).

[9] Tariq Rahman *Language, Ideology, and Power in Pakistan: Language-learning among the*

the language of state before the colonial period, nor during. Yet it *was* associated with cultural production and, as Mir shows, Punjabi literary production flourished in the colonial period despite, and perhaps because of, not benefitting from patronage by the state, where "communalism was promoted, wittingly or unwittingly, by state and civil society," but "other community affiliations" flourished in the *qissā* world.[10] Mir argues that Punjabi reveals "a level of continuity between the pre-colonial and colonial periods not seen in other vernacular literary cultures, a continuity made possible only because of the relative autonomy that colonial language policy itself produced for Punjabi literary and print cultures."[11] It stood somehow free, and flourished as a result.

Yet, there is more to say about the crucial changes as well as continuities that constituted the colonial period, for while Punjabi did provide a medium for the continuance of Punjabi cultural forms like the *qissā,* the language also was engaged towards the production of modern literary works as a part of a global conversation in the late colonial period; it has not only provided a vehicle for the expression of "Punjabi identity." The oldest example of Punjabi prose, according to Sant Singh Sekhon and Kartar Singh Duggal, was Sharda Ram Philauri's 1875 *Sikhāṅ de Rāj dī Vithiā,* which was a historical account of the Sikh kingdoms, which like Rattan Singh Bhangu's 1840 verse history was written on commission for a British agent.[12]

Muslims of Pakistan and North India (Karachi: Oxford University Press, 2002), 381.

[10] Mir *Social Space,* 15, quotes 24.

[11] Mir, *Social Space,* 15.

[12] Sant Singh Sekhon and Kartar Singh Duggal *A History of Punjabi Literature* (New Delhi: Sahitya Akademi, 1992), 105.

The modern form of the novel had emerged by 1898, with Bhai Vir Singh's well-known *Sundari*.[13] It is from this landmark that Punjabi modern literature is usually understood to have proceeded, through figures like Gurbaksh Singh *Preet Larī* (who re-wrote the *qisse*, it should be noted, as modern stories)[14], Mohan Singh, Nanak Singh, and Amrita Pritam and, masters of the short story, Kartar Singh Duggal and Kulwant Singh Virk, among many others. Many of the great prose writers in Urdu in the late colonial, early independence period were of course ethnically Punjabi, though they did not write in the language. Tariq Rahman has argued that up until Partition "Punjabi was not owned by the Muslims" and that "most people... felt that the promotion of Punjabi was a conspiracy to weaken Urdu and, by implication, Muslims."[15] This limited cultural production by Muslims, particularly in the area of modern creative work. But *qisse* certainly were produced by Muslim Punjabi authors in Punjabi in Shahmukhi script in this period, as Mir shows, as was reformist literature. Large numbers of chapbooks were, and have continued to be, produced in Shahmukhi Punjabi.[16] Here too the story is more complicated than has been suggested.[17]

There are thus three broad domains occupied by Punjabi

---

[13] Duggal calls Bhai Vir Singh (1872-1957) the "grand old man of our time," who "upheld the torch of modernism in Punjabi literature." (Sekhon and Duggal, *A History*, 109).

[14] Gurbaksh Singh *Ishak jinhān dī haḍḍīn raciā* (Navayug Publishers, Delhi/Preet Nagar Shaap, Preet Nagar, Amritsar, n.d.).

[15] Rahman, *Language, Ideology*, first quote 397, second 396

[16] Rahman *Language, Ideology*, 422-3.

[17] Rahman himself suggests this: Tariq Rahman *Language and Politics in Pakistan* (Karachi: Oxford University Press, 1996), 198-99.

cultural production in colonial India: as a place for the creative reproduction of existing literary forms, such as the *qissā*, which found a vibrant life in the new print environment of the period; as a language utilized for the expression of religiously marked discourses of debate and reform (and, in alliance with these, historical inquiry and theology) and utilitarian discourses such as astrology or medicine; and for modern literary creation meant to rework tradition (to some extent) and self-consciously utilize new forms.[18] The Punjabi cultural production Mir highlights might be seen as depoliticized, as authors chose to eschew religious identification within an environment where religion was so often infused through the political; at the same time, the choice *not* to engage in religiously marked political positioning is itself a politics, and in the case of modern Punjabi literary production certainly was self-consciously so. It is also the case that Punjabi was utilized for communally charged literature in the period sometimes by the same people who wrote *qisse*, which are the focus of Mir's study and the basis for her claims regarding Punjabi's alternative space (at times one can discern a transition from less to more communally charged literature over the course of authors' lives, but this is not always the case).[19] So these three should not be seen as entirely distinct.

The modern Punjabi literary formation in the post-colonial period both counters and mirrors the complicated position for

---

[18] The three genres identified by Rahman to describe the chapbooks in Pakistan coincide partially with these: religious, romantic, and utilitarian. He does not include modern literary works with these. I do, and group the religious and utilitarian in one category; Rahman *Language, Ideology*, 423. Rahman's category are roughly parallel to those later used by Ayres in her discussion of Punjabi in Pakistan: Alyssa Ayres "Language, the Nation, and Symbolic Capital: The Case of Punjab" in *The Journal of Asian Studies* 67, 3 (August 2008): 917-946; see 932-3.

[19] This comment is based on examination of the Punjabi language guides in the British library.

Punjabi language and literature under the British. The Punjabi language has in particular been implicated in the post-colonial state of India in the search for a platform for the expression of Sikh interests. This was most dramatically visible in the fight for a linguistically (and culturally) defined Punjabi *sūba* or province, which, as Paul Brass rightly noted early on, can only be understood in the context of the post-colonial state of India in relation to the Hindi movement and already existing issues around the imbrication of language and religious identity in the Hindi/Urdu controversy (which had already expressed itself in the effort to displace Urdu as the language of the Province of Punjab in 1882).[20] In Punjab in the colonial period, Rahman argues, "the Urdu-Punjabi controversy was an extension of the Urdu-Hindi controversy.[21] As Paul Brass has noted, "the regional languages of the north have been able to survive against the inroads of Hindi only where they have been useful as symbols in the struggles of minority peoples, such as Muslims and Sikhs, whose demands have not been primarily linguistic." [22] This is the dynamic that marked the movement for the

---

[20] Paul Brass *Language, Religion, and Politics in North India* (New York: Cambridge University Press, 1974), 287. As Brass notes, "the competition between the Hindi movement and the other languages of Punjab, including Punjabi,... [had] been in progress for nearly a century." Brass, *Language*, 292.

[21] Rahman, *Language, Ideology*, 395. He argues that "the political need of the time, as perceived by Muslim leaders in the heat of the Pakistan movement, was to insist on a common Muslim identity" that Urdu played a major part in, although this is less convincing an argument for Punjab given that the Pakistan movement was successful there so late--we must keep Mir's portrait of Punjabi Shahmukhi literary production in view here.

[22] Brass *Language* 297. Narang rightly argues that, indeed, many of the dynamics of the Hindu right in India today must be understood in relation to Hindu activism in Punjab and the communal climate of the state. (A. S. Narang "Movement for the Punjabi-Speaking State" 243-266, in *Five Punjabi Centuries: Polity, Economy, Society, and Culture, 1500-1990* Indu Banga, ed. (New Delhi: Manohar, 1997), 253.)

Punjabi *sūba* in post-colonial India: its cultural and religious as well as linguistic character, although its linguistic character was explicitly at the forefront.[23] It is generally accepted that the 1961 census, which was used to determine the boundaries of the Punjabi language state, did not reflect the actual mother tongues of the speakers of Hindi and Punjabi in the then Punjab; instead Hindus were encouraged by the Arya Samaj and other organizations to declare their mother tongue to be Hindi, and Punjabi came to be more and more identified with Sikhs alone.[24] Thus, the Punjabi state was framed as a linguistic space, but language was determined to reflect religious affiliation; indeed, Brass argues that language and the Gurmukhi script are one of three major constituting forces of Sikh identity overall.[25] The quest for a Punjabi speaking state is not unique, of course, in the post-colonial state and the process of linguistic reorganization is continuing today; the state of Andhra Pradesh was granted in 1952 and in 1959, the Congress High Command decided to split Bombay into two states—Maharastra and Gujarat (and as we know, such changes have continued).[26] The formation of the Punjabi language state, however, did not take place until late in the early period of reorganization, in the wake of the Indian-Pakistan war of 1965.[27]

---

[23] A member of the Akali Dal Working Committee has related that the Committee was advised by Dr. Ambedkar to frame their argument in linguistic terms, so that "you can have a Sikh State in the cloak of 'Punjabi Suba'" (Quoted in Narang, "Movement," 252).

[24] Brass, *Language,* 293-4. Manipulation in the census was an issue from 1911 on; see Brass *Language* 292.

[25] Brass, *Language* 278.

[26] Narang, "Movement," 259. J.S. Grewal, *Sikhs of the Punjab* (Cambridge: Cambridge University Press, 1990), 188.

[27] Prime Minister Indira Gandhi was said to be in search of support for her

The political ties of the Punjabi literary world are no surprise; the history of modern vernacular literary production in South Asia is deeply tied to a broader history of leftist and progressive politics. As Priyamvada Gopal has described, "the historical conjuncture from the early 1930s to the years immediately after independence made possible a range of historical tasks or, at the very least, a *perception* that it would be possible--and necessary--to undertake certain kinds of radical endeavors"[28]; this was the founding crucible of the Progressive Writers Association (founded in 1936), with a commitment to critical engagement with and reconstruction of the past and present, towards the production of a new future that would exceed the confines of the present.[29] This occurred without, at least at first, a strict adherence to leftist party politics, although these did explicitly shape organizations and individuals increasingly over time.[30] Such commitments have continued in the post-Independence period, particularly in Pakistan, demonstrating the inadequacy of Alyssa Ayres' explanation of the Punjabi language and literature movement in Pakistan as an example of a uniquely non-nationalist and symbolic linguistic project. As Kalra and Butt persuasively assert, "It is a lack of an analysis that takes into account class, which misdirects much of the research on the Punjabi movement in West Punjab,"[31]

---

leadership in supporting it. (Narang, "Movement," 262-3).

[28] Priyamvada Gopal *Literary Radicalism in India: Gender, Nation, and the Transition to Independence* (London: Routledge, 2005), 22.

[29] Gopal *Literary Radicalism*, 14.

[30] Gopal *Literary Radicalism*, 17-18, 20.

[31] Virinder S. Kalra and Waqas M. Butt "'In one hand a pen, in the other a gun: Punjabi language radicalism in Punjab, Pakistan" in *South Asian History and Culture* (September 2013): 1-16; see pg 4.

where left organization and activism is central. Ayres errs in subsuming the political into the national alone and in separating the symbolic and the political, as Kalra and Butt note.[32]

Punjabi literature today is very much both local and global, the product of a major and self-consciously transnational language and literary movement and simultaneously rooted in very particular local institutions and concerns, exemplified by the Sahit Sabhas and other related organizations that are as common in the countryside of Punjab as they are a central part of the Punjabi Diaspora. Many are deeply linked to progressive and/or leftist politics. At the same time, the Punjabi movement is deeply literary. It exhibits deep ties to Punjabi language literary production in East Punjab and the Punjabi Diaspora. Connections between the two Punjabs are tenuous at times, because of the difficulty of travel between the two states and the use of different scripts, although some members of both literary communities do read across the script divide. On the Web, Punjabi language writers remain in contact across the physical border through the well-known website apna.org, as well as a Facebook page called "*Kitāb Trinjan*," in honour of a Punjabi language bookshop in Lahore, on Punjabi writers and translators maintained by Dublin-based Mahmood Awan, who writes about Punjabi literature in English for Pakistan's *The News*. Amarjit Chandan, the well-known poet based in London who has been most active in the Punjabi literary Diaspora in engaging with an English-speaking audience through translation, also has strong ties in West Punjab as well as East. Such individuals demonstrate the deeply transnational nature of modern Punjabi literary production. This has been enhanced recently by the founding of an international Prize for Punjabi

---

[32] Kalra and Butt "'In one hand a pen," 6, 15.

literature, which held its inaugural awards ceremony in October 2014 in Vancouver Canada.[33]

Placing Punjabi Diaspora literature

Yet where do we place Punjabi and other vernacular literatures written *outside* of India? As the rich literature in Punjabi produced in places like greater Vancouver, Canada attests, that which is vernacular is cosmopolitan in the broadest sense. It is as global as it is local, and this is what we must attend to before we accept the conventional formulation of writing the diaspora in languages like Punjabi. The works in the landmark collection of Canadian short stories in Punjabi, *Kathā Kaneḍa (A Collection of Canadian Punjabi Short Stories),* published in 2000, for instance, are singularly concerned with the experience of Punjabis in Canada, in complex relationship with lives and experiences in India.[34] They critique the racism and other challenges faced by Punjabis in Canada, but also hierarchical and abusive relations *within* Punjabi and Punjabi-Canadian society, in the present and in the past, such as caste and gender discrimination.

The stories produce time alongside of place, and in dynamic relation to language. Located in Vancouver, in BC, they describe an ongoing present that may be connected to other times or places (namely, the Indian Punjab) but which is always simultaneously new and reworked. Recent works such as Sadhu Binning's book *No more 'Watanoṅ Dūr',* a collection of his poems, have articulated forcefully this re-imagination of time

---

[33] The Prize is called the Dhahan Prize for Punjabi Literature. The author of this article chaired the Advisory Committee for the Prize from 2012 to 2014.

[34] Binning, Sadhu and Sukhwant Hundal, eds. *Kathā Kaneḍā (A Collection of Canadian Punjabi Short Stories)* Ludhiana: Chetna Prakashan, 2000).

and space partially by bridging a linguistic gap alongside a geographical one, by presenting translations into English alongside Punjabi originals; Fauzia Rafiq's *Skeena* (2011) provides another example, with its "transcreation" of Shahmukhi Punjabi (in the Perso-Arabic script, as utilized in the Pakistani Punjab), Gurmukhi Punjabi (as used in the Indian Punjab), and English versions.[35] What this shows dramatically is that that which is vernacular--that is, what is conventionally viewed in India in local and limited terms, and as prior, as "non-English"--is worldly and cosmopolitan in the broadest sense and must be defined at a complex intersection of time, space, and language. It is as global as it is local, and this is what we must attend to before we accept the conventional formulation of writing in the diaspora as subservient to a relationship with the homeland.

Sukhwant Hundal's *"Jūthī Plaiṭ,"* or "Soiled plate," from *Kathā Kaneḍā,* for example, gives a compelling account of one woman's experience of an abusive marriage, where she describes herself with the phrase used for the title. Hundal wrote the story after hearing exactly those denigrating words of a husband to his wife that are uttered at the climax of the story, after the husband reveals to his friends the intimate details of their wedding night. The story does refer to a past in the Punjab, neither idealized nor demonized, but in relation to an urgent present, captured in this phrase, which encapsulates everything about the relationship of this man and woman. Surjeet Kalsey's *"Melo dī Kahānī,"* "The Story of Melo" describes the strength of a woman choosing to leave behind an abusive

---

[35] Sadhu Binning. *No More Watnaoṅ Dūr (Far from the homeland).* (Toronto: TSAR, 1994); Fauzia Rafique *Skeena* (Surrey, BC, Canada: Libros Libertad, 2011). This "transcreation" process was described by Rafique to the author over email, 2011.

marriage, and the difficulty of doing so. Harpreet Sekha's *"Vickārlī Saṛak"* or "The Road in Between," provides a portrait of the persistence of caste hierarchies in Canada, even when challenges to such relations are articulated in India. A subtle relationship is thus staked out between behaviors here and those in Punjab: Punjab is as much the source of challenge and change as of tradition. In Sekha's piece, for example, the inspiration for countering caste is derived from a particular politics articulated first in Punjab, not in diaspora. To give an example from outside that collection of stories, Sadhu Binning's *"Jaṭ dā Puṭṭ"* or "Son of a Jaṭ," provides a similar vivid portrait of progressive politics in Punjab. Binning describes how the "new" space of Canada reinscribes—indeed, rewrites entirely— experiences from Punjab such that political and personal decisions *there* are scripted in the new *here* as issues of 'honor' and 'tradition', denuded of the local politics that had animated them in the Punjab. The danger of the diaspora, in this vision, is the absence of a grounded politics in the now and an idealized past that goes unchallenged.

The dynamic exchange between Punjab and Canada portrayed in such stories, therefore, is not nostalgic or simplistic. The past is not Punjab, the present Canada. The two are imbricated in complex power relations in an unfolding present. For example, the story *"Andar Baiṭhe Dar"* or "A fear that sits inside," by Harpreet Singh Sekha (not from *Kathā Kaneḍā*, but a single-authored collection of stories) is deeply personal and local as well as global in its orientation, weaving remembrance of the post-Babri Masjid riots in Mumbai with the experience of post-9/11 New York and the rising spectre of anti-Muslim bias crimes in North America into a deeply transnational and yet local tapestry. The narrator of the story, which was written by a Sikh male, is a Muslim woman. And of course these are only some of the literary positions taken by authors in BC; others are far less politically oriented, and more concerned with form and emotional expression. The political and the personal are, however, persistent themes. Another example of the capacious reach of Punjabi-language writers in Canada is the portrayal of village life in the story *"Mukkharā Cann Vargā"* or "A Face like the Moon," from *Kathā Kaneda.* This story denies any simple characterization of home and abroad, as the central character struggles to face the reality of his mother's relationship with a man who is not her husband, in his village in Punjab. Her husband (whom he thought was his father, but may not have been) spent most of his life in Canada. Where is the local here? Where is "tradition"? Homeland is not the past, and the continuing present constitutes both the triumph and the struggles of both diaspora and homeland.

Temporality and locality in the making of a diaspora history

Vigocā, a recent novel by prominent Sikh author from greater Vancouver, Jarnail Singh Sekha, published in 2012, provides a striking example of the complex interaction of time and place in Punjabi fiction, emerging as a novel out of the act of story-telling: a mother sitting her son down to relate the past. That narrative of the past is always disrupted by the present, and the past is not "homeland" in relation to the present of diaspora; the linearity of time is disrupted, and the chapters alternate between past and present in exchange. So too are exchanges between India and Canada, portrayed as a continual unfolding, not a past and present. Time and place are, simply, fluid.

24

Vigocā means lack or want. There are two times when this term is mentioned explicitly in the story. The first is when a woman who marries a man with a young boy is told that her job is to make sure this child does not feel the lack or *vigocā* of not having his mother (who died giving birth to him) (166) The second is the want felt by a mother, at the loss of her daughter, who left the family because of their lack of support for her desire to marry a Punjabi Canadian man of a lower caste background than she (a Jat) (302). But in a sense the entire story is one of loss: the loss of beloved family members, across generations, in the building up of a long history of place and time. At the same time, it is a story that is full, overfull perhaps, of history and place-over-time: its very structure and substance denies "lack." It is indeed in many senses a fictional history, a grand narrative in the broadest sense: a history of a family, and of two nations, Canada and India, and the evolving and constant relationship formed between them through migration and exchange.

The central figure of the story is Bobby, an Indo-Canadian gang leader, and his mother, Sarabjit. It is she who attempts to instill in her son a sense of his own family and past, and its ongoing importance in the present, through story-telling. The narration of the past is thus an argument, directed at guiding Sarabjit's son out of his violent activities, through the past and into a new now. The history of the Indo-Canadian community is fully narrated: the early pioneers, the Komagata Maru incident. The relentless experience of racism in the 1960s and 1970s, and the urgency of that experience in the 1980s. We hear of Operation Bluestar and the Air India bombing; of the Indo Canadian Workers Association and their battle to fight for the rights of workers. We also are told of First Nations history, presented as a counter history to the European dominated narration of the Canadian national story (220). These stories are woven through chapters that describe Bobby's rise to power in the world of drug smuggling, and his eventual coming to terms with the price he has paid for that power. By denying a linear progression from past to present, and instead interweaving the past through the present and meeting the two in the future (past that point where the novel begins, thus also denying the simple trope of flashback), the novel destabilizes any simplistic configuration of time and place, and any direct trajectory from here to there. India is a constant companion of Canada in this book; neither is it lost or found, left or longed for.. The two are as joined and continually present, as they provide the source of life and history to characters that travel through these spaces, through the past and into the present, but also always moving back.

This travel is also linguistic. The novel portrays its characters as speaking in English (even though it is entirely in Punjabi), demonstrating linguistically a move *from* one language to another. But this move does not designate a fundamental shift: characters are deeply engaged with their families and cultures, and the sense of change that is thereby articulated is not absolute, it is *linguistic*. (Language, then, is not a stand-in for culture here, evoking the sensibility that informs the bilingual creations mentioned above that embrace Punjabi and English alongside temporal and spatial flux..) The return of Punjabi appears explicitly toward the end of the novel, when Bobby confesses to his uncle his desire to leave the drug trade—after for the first time admitting his involvement. What drives him to this decision? It is the realization of the pain that the violence of that world brings to families. He describes the state of the family of his friend, Anup, after his friend's death. His uncle notes *"bilkul terī māṅ dā hāl vī ajehā hī hoṇā ai, je tainūṅ kujh ho giā*

That is exactly the state your mother would be in, if something happened to you," and Bobby replies, in Punjabi, *"maiṅ jāṇḍā* I know." Of course, the entire novel is written in Punjabi, but this is when we are made aware by the author that all dialogue (particularly with Bobby) has been actually been taking place in English among the characters, until Bobby uncharacteristically speaks in Punjabi here. The use of Punjabi represents Bobby's full recognition of his role in his family, and the responsibility he bears for his mother in the fullest terms. It is at this point in the novel, too--indeed, with these words in Punjabi--that the past and present meet, and there are no more shifts in time. We are in the today, in Punjabi, and it is one where Bobby must accept the problematic reality of his present.

Where and when is Punjabi diaspora literature?

Punjabi language diaspora literature is located at various intersections. It is in many senses rooted in Punjab, given that most of those who write in Punjabi in Canada today were born in South Asia (few Canadian-born Punjabi Canadians have started writing in Punjabi, but there are a few, such as Kwantlen Polytechnic University instructor Ranbir Johal), but at the same time is fundamentally Canadian literature, marked by a the play of language that intersects with the play of time and place in complex ways. Locality, in this sense, does matter. But that too is a problem, since Punjabi as a language does not have the broad reach of English in Canada. Translation is one way to reach local audiences who do not speak Punjabi, but there are dangers in translation. We see in a recent essay by Anushiya Sivanarayan how a Tamil text translated into English is flattened to speak solely for a Dalit liberatory politics, such that "the personal, the peculiar, the elements that refuse to be placed under the heading of a conscious liberatory rhetoric are left out."[36] Texts thus are made to provide cultural representations to a larger public, simultaneously homogenizing world cultures[37] and, as noted in several of the essays in Iyer and Zare's recent volume on the language debates in India, providing "cultural ambassadors" that "offer a readily translatable Idiots' Guide to South Asia and South Asian Immigrants… or a Cliffs-notes version of the subcontinent."[38] Indeed, such a critique was voiced at *Skeena*'s recent release event in Vancouver, that as a Pakistani Muslim author Rafique is relegated to acting as a "native informant"; there is certainly no doubt that this was how her book was interpreted by some of those commenting on it at that event: as a window into a Pakistani and/or Muslim world, rather than into her vision as an individual writer. Yet the deeply humanist sensibilities of works like *Vigocā* and *Skeena* require that such a risk be taken, to reach beyond such a reading, and it is also the case that every work is very much embedded within the positioning of the author, so the connection between work and identity is persistent.

Binning's story *"Jatt dā Putt"* provides an example of the difficulties of translation: his is a critique of multiple layers of Punjabi society, both in India and in Canada, and one that would not be easily translated. How does one explain the tensions the protagonist faces with the challenges of political activism in India, and what is at stake in resorting to a defense of *izzat* in Canada as a way to assert Punjabi male authority, against the backdrop of an earlier political failure? *"Sabhiacār da*

---

[36] Iyer and Zare, *Other Tongues*, 139.

[37] Iyer and Zare, *Other Tongues*, 152.

[38] Iyer and Zare, *Other Tongues*, 82 first quote, 47 second.

rakkhwālā," a short story from Harprit Singh Sekha's collection "*Bī Jī Muskarā Pae*" provides another example of what is beyond translation. In this story, Sekhā challenges readers to consider the double standards that hold for women outside of and within the Punjabi community. One of the characters of the story—the protector of culture of the title of the story—claims to take part in daring sexual escapades with white women. Punjabi women, on the other hand, need to be protected—and controlled. When challenged on this by the narrator of the story, the character calls those women as being from a lesser community, unworthy. The ability to read Punjabi, in this context, provides a protective environment in which this real critique--which does reflect perceptions of white women among South Asian men--can take place. Yet translation might undermine the political import and even viability of such writing, if the full valences of it are not available to the reader. The politics of such works cannot be "explained" away with the addition of cultural information to make such a text accessible to a wider audience. This story in some senses therefore needs to remain untranslated.

The experience of time and place that is contained in such works, perhaps, also eludes translation. This, I think, is where the true experience of Diaspora is expressed in literary and fictional terms: in relation to time. As Benzi Zhang has noted, "the earlier conceptualizations of home based on a singular location are no longer adequate to describe the new dimensions and transformations of home, which has been re-versed in diaspora not as a 'felicitous space' of living, but rather a process of (be-)coming."[39] By the end of Sekha's *Vigocā* the reader

---

[39] Benzi Zhang "The Politics of Rehoming: Asian Diaspora Poetry in Canada" in *College Literature* 31, 1 (2004): 103-125; see pp. 103-4. Zhang also suggests the need to think of diaspora in temporal as well as locative terms, but this idea is not fully developed and is linear in its trajectory; see pg. 112.

achieves the present, through various engagements with the past, and also re-enters the Punjabi language (having traversed the story through Punjabi, of course, throughout, but really in English, we find out). The diasporic subject in this fictional mode is always becoming, as a figure of time, and always tied to a past and a language that continues to be made and is un-done. This temporal and linguistic flux is perhaps expressed fully in fiction, which allows for the narration of a story in simultaneous expression, as unfolding presents separated and joined only by time, and in the process of merging. I would argue, however, that in this sense the fictional perhaps best represents the real: the temporal continuities that comprise us, and our indebtedness to a past that is never done.

3

A(T) HOME IN THE WORLD: NEOLIBERALIZING
INDIAN NATIONAL IDENTITY IN A GLOBAL ERA.

RINA VERMA WILLIAMS

Introduction

The concept of diaspora contains embedded within itself—
indeed is constituted by—the concept of home: home is that
(place) from which diasporas are removed. In this sense,
diaspora makes no sense without a home from which to be
removed. We think of diasporas most usually in terms of a
national home and a conception of a corresponding national
identity; though the concept of diasporas can refer to other
(types of) communities as well, such as the African diaspora, or
the Jewish diaspora.[1] In this essay I will focus on the concept of

---

[1] I am grateful to Danielle Bessett for pointing this out.

national identities as viewed through the lens of Indian national identity. In an era of unceasing circulation and flow of people, capital, cultures and identities across national borders, it seems facile and easy to assume that national identity must inevitably wither away. Scholars have spilled much ink asking whether, or how, globalization spells the end of national identity. In this essay I argue that rather than withering away in an era of neoliberal globalization, Indian national identity instead has itself become mobile, diasporic, neoliberalized: reconfigured, reinvented and adapted to be 'at home' in the world but still to be 'a home' in the world.[2]

Simply to argue that nationalism has globalized itself is insufficient. In critically important senses national identity in general, and certainly Indian national identity in particular, was always already globalized. The very concept of India as a national entity was constructed in the context of, and in resistance to, colonial rule (Khilnani 1999). British conceptions of themselves as a nation and a people were forged in the crucible of difference from the colonial other. Scholars of nationalism and of globalization have long known that globalization did not wipe out the relevance of national borders and boundaries; national identity has reasserted itself in countless, often violent and destructive ways as ethnic, religious, or even civilizational conflict. What, then, is new or noteworthy or distinctive about the globalization of nationalism today? I argue that globalization today—and correspondingly, the globalization of nationalism today—is marked by neoliberalism. In this historical moment in which the imposition or

---

[2] This is a play on words from the title of Rabindranath Tagore's classic 1916 novel *The Home and the World*.

assumption of core tenets of neoliberalism has spread around the globe, the construction of national identity can be seen to have adapted to this context: national identity itself has taken on key characteristics of neoliberalism in this particular era of globalization, and it is these neoliberal characteristics that make this era of globalization unique.

I trace evolving conceptions of Indian national identity over time. I contrast Indian national identity before and after the transitional period of the 1980s-90s, when India underwent/undertook economic reforms and liberalization, opening itself nationally and economically to greater participation in and integration with the global economic order. Prior to this transitional period, Indian national identity was more closed and insular, a more conventional conception of national identity that was linked to the power of the state and building a collective sense of Indian identity. Since this transitional period of the 1980s-90s, Indian national identity has expanded into the world in such a way as to establish its presence in the global arena while retaining the core essence of a national identity that constructs itself as innately unique and even inherently superior. Unmoored, no longer anchored to a state, a community, or even a geographic terrain, Indian national identity has itself become mobile and diasporic, joining the very unceasing flows and circulations of the globalization that we once speculated might destroy it.

I trace these permutations of Indian national identity before and after the transitional period of the mid-1980s to the early 1990s through two interwoven narratives. I narrate a pre-transitional conception of Indian national identity through my own personal experiences as a scholar of Indian origin, born in

India, who grew up in the United States. Then I illustrate the contours of a post-transitional—neoliberal, globalized—conception of Indian national identity through portrayals of Indians, the west, and Indian national identity in popular Bollywood cinema. Though I refer to other films, my primary analysis is focused on the recent blockbuster hit *Yeh Jawaani Hai Diwaani* (*YJHD*, 2013; 'This Youth Is Madness').[3]

I begin by reviewing evolving scholarly debates about globalization and neoliberalism that form the theoretical underpinning of my argument, and briefly discuss the Indian economic reforms and liberalization of the 1980s and early 1990s. I then discuss my own personal experiences of Indian national identity prior to the transitional period, followed by an analysis of Bollywood films to illustrate the contours of a neoliberalized, post-transitional conception of Indian national identity as portrayed in these films. I conclude by briefly considering some of the implications of the neoliberalization of national identity more broadly.

Context and Transition: Globalization and Neoliberalism in Theory and in Fact

The earliest globalization literature often argued national identity and the power of nation-states would 'whither away' or become irrelevant as globalization expanded (Ohmae 1995; Strange 1996). Subsequent, more critical waves of literature have acknowledged that this was not the case. A first wave of critique argued that far from destroying national identity, the forces of globalization seemed instead to be propagating some

---

[3] I must thank my family in India—and especially my cousin, Anamika Sahay—for bringing this film to my attention. I'm sure when she did so she didn't suspect I'd end up including it in an academic analysis of Indian nationalism!

national identities (or cultures) at the expense of others. In particular, this line of critique suggested that globalization comprised the imposition of western (often US) values and cultures at the expense of the cultures and national identities of poorer and developing nations. Recent analyses have acknowledged that globalization is not a matter of simple or unidirectional imposition of western norms or values, and have traced forms of resistance as well (Jafar 2013: xi).

Since this earlier literature, scholars have evolved more nuanced analyses of the phenomena that constitute globalization. Some have questioned whether globalization is in fact a new phenomenon, suggesting that colonialism may be considered the first—or at least a very early—form of globalization. In this sense, globalization can be traced back to marxist analyses of international trade and imperialism brought forward in neocolonial forms of global capitalism and multi- and transnational corporations (Turner 2010: 3).

Globalization studies have focused on economic, cultural and political aspects of globalization. Ultimately, globalization has been elusive to define, with many definitions reverting to some form of argument about quantity, pace, and scope of phenomena (such as migration, technology and mobility) that are acknowledged to have pre-existed whenever globalization was supposed to have begun. That is, scholars of globalization seem often to argue that it constitutes 'more' or a lot more, a lot faster, of something(s) that were already extant. Thus one scholar has noted that a definition of globalization involves

> some consensus that globalization involves the *compression* of time and space, the *increased* interconnectivity of human groups, the *increased volume* of the exchange of commodities,

people, and ideas, and finally the emergence of various forms of global consciousness (Turner 2010: 5; emphases mine)

In terms of chronology, those who argue that there is something new or different about the current era of globalization tend to focus on the post-World War II or post-Cold War periods as marking new departures for globalization (Lechner 2004: 1-2). A prime example is Arjun Appadurai's argument that a new era of globalization from about the mid-1970s has been marked by two characteristics in particular: first, the proliferation of electronic media has greatly expanded the speed and range at which images and events can (be) spread. Second, waves of migration and population mobility—whether more or less forced—have grown to greater heights than at any previous time in history. This combination of moving images and de-territorialized viewers created what Appadurai called 'diasporic public spheres' (1996: 4).

The most recent analyses of globalization have noted that borders and nations still matter, citing greater rates and speeds of cross-border interactions. They note that globalization is not the same as westernization or homogenization. While many traditional studies focused on macro level institutions and entities of globalization, the most thoughtful recent analyses have recognized individuals as the engines of globalization and those who are affected by its processes: in this sense a key aspect of globalization is the material conditions of people's everyday lives. Globalization is defined in terms of its (always increased or increasing) rate, speed, and flow (de Casanova 2013: xviii-ix). Since the events of 9/11 in the United States, globalization theory has returned to the ideas of (re)territorialization of nation states, leaving behind prior discussions of 'a borderless world and the decline of the nation-state.' Scholars now examine not just the fluidities and movements produced by globalization but also the enclosures and entrapments it produces. If mobility is a resource, then unequal access to it becomes a form of containment—whether physical or biological, as in forms of surveillance (Turner 2010: 19-20).

Scholars have also argued that the form taken by globalization since the 1980s is a specific one: that of neoliberalism. Neoliberalism can be identified as a primarily economic phenomenon with critically important political aspects. After the global economic crises of the 1970s, 'an entirely new breed of liberals sought a way forward by reviving the old doctrine of classical liberalism under the novel conditions of globalization' (Steger 2010: 9). Given the nature of the crises of the 1970s, the way forward sought was specifically to be capitalist and anti-collective/socialist/marxist in any sense; hence neoliberalism grew out of, and remains tied intimately with, a need to oppose statism or planned economies of any sort.

Economic neoliberalism is associated with a core cluster of policies including the promotion of free markets, conservative monetary and fiscal policy, deregulation, privatization, and the lowering or elimination of trade barriers. Its primary patrons and champions in the 1980s were US President Ronald Reagan and British Prime Minister Margaret Thatcher; in the 1990s, US President Bill Clinton and British Prime Minister Tony Blair were associated with a second wave of neoliberalism (Harvey 2005). In Asia, neoliberalism manifested differently in various countries: China began a controlled turn to neoliberalism in the 1970s, while in India the turn began a bit later, in 1984, following a period of essentially socialist state-led development policies from the time of independence in 1947. In Africa and Latin America, neoliberal policies manifested as structural adjustment policies (SAPs) imposed on struggling economies by the International Monetary Fund and the World Bank—SAPs generally included requirements of spending cuts (most especially in social programs), currency devaluation, and the usual cocktail of deregulation, privatization, and dismantling of protectionist tariffs and trade barriers in order to allow western capital greater access to these markets (Steger 2010).

The political aspects of neoliberalism derive fairly directly from its economic aspects, constituting a cluster of factors closely interlinked with each other. For the purposes of assessing changes in conceptions of nationalism and national identity, two of the most relevant political aspects of neoliberalism are:

a) the demise of statism or conceptions of state-led development or even welfare statism. At its most extreme, this comes even to the denial of any important role for the state in any aspect of society or the economy whatsoever, beyond minimal functions of ensuring order and protecting and guaranteeing the freest possible operation of the free market; and

b) the corresponding rise and even fetishization of individualism and individual freedom. This has resulted in the virtual abnegation of all state/institutional or collective responsibility for anything and the transference of that responsibility onto individuals.

As such, 'neoliberal projects are not simply defined by the removal of state intervention, but rather inaugurate new indirect forms of power that seek to extend the enterprise form to all spheres of life and encourage the production of self-governing individuals' (von Schnitzler 2008: 474).

Though it can manifest politically in different ways, the core economic goal of neoliberalism is the establishment of a single global free market, and in this sense economic neoliberalism stands philosophically apart from strains of economic nationalism. At a glance, one might infer that neoliberalism has little room for nationalism in the form of loyalty to national communities: indeed, the vision of a single global free market seems precisely the negation of national boundaries and borders. But in fact both Reagan and Thatcher retained strong nationalistic strains in their rhetoric and policies. Both remained attached to nationalism as translated into a vision of Anglo-American civilizational values of political liberty, free market commerce, and love of country (Steger 2010: 45). And for all the anti-statist rhetoric, it remains the case that both Reagan and Thatcher 'depended, paradoxically, on the muscle of state-imposed neoliberal reforms' and 'the rise of neoliberalism would have been impossible without strong government action' (Steger 2010: 49).

Such paradoxes suggest that neoliberal globalization retains a place and a function for nationalism after all. Conventional conceptions of nationalism were linked inextricably to states and state power, and in turn to geography and territories (Gellner 1983; Smith 1986). Even Benedict Anderson's nations as 'imagined communities' were dependent on states and maps of territories and geographies, (as well as print media) to imagine themselves (Anderson 1983). In the postcolonial context, nationalism was understood as the building of a collective sense of identity by and for the state so that countries would be more governable: increasing crises of ethnic conflict and political instability were read as failures to establish nationalism (Horowitz 2000).

Scholars have long agreed that in an era of globalization, nationalism has not been erased. But its forms have changed: the ceaseless and rapid movement of media images and populations produces a delinking of sorts of national identities from states and territories/geographies. This delinking, this freeing of nationalism from its anchors enables it to free-float globally, and in the process nations become 'culturalized' (Appadurai 1996): marked, defined, and identified primarily by and as cultural formations rather than political formations in the conventional senses outlined above. National identities in the current era have become detached and separated from the conventional functions that nationalism performed, at least in theory: the cultivation of group identity and loyalty, collective solidarity with a broader, imagined community, and the linking of that community identity and loyalty to a state and territory.

The new neoliberal nationalism breaks both these ties of conventional nationalism—in a word, newer neoliberal forms of globally circulating national identities are marked by the two key characteristics of neoliberalism identified above: a de-emphasis on statism and the prioritization of individual rather than collective forms of identification. First, as Appadurai identified, national cultures and imaginations have become mobile along with the populations that carry them. In this way, nationalisms now travel and traverse global spaces such that they cease to be necessarily linked to the states and territories whence they originated. Thus Indian immigrants in the US watch Indian television and movies on satellite channels, while British ex-pats attend cricket games in South Africa.

Second, new neoliberal formations of nationalism become individualized: nationalism and national identity come to be attached to individuals rather than collectivities, moving with individuals wherever they go. It no longer becomes necessary for an individual to be or live physically in Germany or with other Germans, for example, to carry a legitimate and legitimately recognized sense of German identity. Nationalism becomes no longer primarily about creating a collective or group identity, the identity of the nation itself. Rather, nationalism becomes an individual identity—how a person identifies as Chinese or French, for example, or even indeed whether and how others identify people in national ways.

These trajectories of nationalism can be traced by contrasting shifting conceptions of Indian national identity before and after the transitional period of 1984-1996. Until the 1980s, India's political economy was by and large a closed one: the explicit goal of the mixed economy established by Jawaharlal Nehru, a leader of the independence movement and the first Prime Minister of independent India, was self-sufficiency. This meant a mix of public and private ownership of economic enterprises in which heavy industry was under government control, while small consumer industries were under private ownership. The system tilted toward a socialist economy, guided by a series of Five-Year Plans and featuring heavy government regulation of prices, wages, and employment. In practice, this meant little trade with other countries and no export-oriented industrialization or growth policies. This approach served to free India for many decades from the grip of external debt in which so many postcolonial countries quickly became entangled.

This political-institutional and economic self-sufficiency began to crack open in the mid-1980s under Prime Minister Rajiv Gandhi (Nehru's grandson), who initiated the process of liberalization in response to the foreign-currency crisis he faced.[4] Balance of payments problems began in 1985, and India faced a full-blown foreign currency crisis by 1990. The resolution required an emergency loan from the International Monetary Fund (IMF)—and the collateral was the country's entire gold reserves. The crisis jump-started India's economic liberalization process, which involved slowly opening up the country's economy to the world and even more slowly dismantling the maze of heavy-handed government regulation of the economy that had come to be known as the Permit Raj.

This transitional period that I mark from 1984 until 1996 corresponded substantially with two Congress Party governments associated with India's economic liberalization process—that of Prime Minister Rajiv Gandhi from 1984 to 1989, and P. V. Narasimha Rao from 1991 to 1996. The former is widely understood as having taken the early steps that initiated the reform process, while the latter is seen as having deepened the reforms, cementing the process and making it irreversible. This period represents a moment of convergence between international and domestic Indian trends: this is the time period both identified by Appadurai as marking a new era

---

[4] The literature on India's economic reforms is vast and continues to grow. For a start, see Sachs 2000; Bardhan 2010; Nayar 2014.

of globalization and the wide spread of neoliberal tenets around the world, as well as the time of the transformation and initiation of India into this new world order. As such, my construction of phases before and after this transitional period is deliberate, but is not meant to suggest that either period followed any mold of nationalism perfectly or completely; nor that any processes of transition, reform, or liberalization are linear or complete.

What political and economic liberalization has brought in its wake, I suggest, is the demise of a sort of national-cultural self-sufficiency in India and the neoliberalization of national identity. Along with the economic opening and an opening up of the country to globalization and internationalization came an opening up of the country's national identity to the world. In the next section I trace a pre-transitional form of Indian national identity, prior to 1984, marked by a lingering conventional conception of national identity narrated through the lens of my own personal experience(s) as an Indian immigrant growing up in the US whilst maintaining strong cultural and familial ties in India.

The Personal: (My Own) Pre-Transitional National Identities

My own status and positionality as an Indian immigrant to the United States has been fairly unique, as each personal narrative is; the timing of my parents' immigration was unusual even if the story of their move was less so. My father came to the US in 1964 to get his PhD in electrical engineering from UC Berkeley, leaving my mother already pregnant with me back in India. When I was 11 months old my mother and I traveled to the US to join my father. Thus we came to the US just before the 1965 opening up of immigration policy that led to subsequent, much larger waves of immigration.

Through high school and college (which for me constituted the 1980s), we visited India frequently enough, and maintained family ties closely enough, to feel a strong sense of connection to India. What I never felt was that India had a strong sense of connection to me. That is, India did not always feel like a place that had a place for someone like me: someone who left early and young and grew up her whole life in the west.

These oddities of time and space in my own personal narrative resulted in my status as something of an oddity when I would return to India to visit.[5] Any number of issues of identity arose: was I really Indian or really American? By what standard or measure was I counted as less Indian than cousins who had grown up in India but whose mothers were European (German and Irish)? What conception of national identity would let someone who is ethnically 'only half Indian' be considered, and consider themselves to be, 'more Indian' than someone who is fully ethnically Indian?

These issues—what I came to feel and understand as the culpability of my American-ness and uncertainty of my Indian-ness—also appeared around the time that I reached marriageable age. Unlike many first-generation immigrants, my parents were forward thinking enough to not distinguish between the educational and career futures of their daughters

---

[5] It is worth noting at this point, perhaps in passing, that for the sake of the ideas I'm trying to think through here, I'm entirely ignoring the reverse side of this story—which of course is that America equally had no place for me either. Thus I do not address in this paper my corresponding and often ongoing status as an oddity in the US.

and their son. But probably like many first generation immigrants, they were perhaps not culturally, emotionally, or chronologically removed enough from India to imagine that I wouldn't have an arranged marriage. They cast their nets far and wide in a pre-internet era. Much of the searching was done through personal connections, so I came, as it were, highly recommended: a good girl from a good family who had retained strong cultural and emotional ties to India. To my knowledge, no overtures or proposals were made that were rejected outright; but in some muddled way I came to realize that we weren't playing in the top leagues of this sport—that somehow, for some reason, we had been relegated to the B-leagues. We figured out circuitously that my having grown up in America was a liability. None of the really good boys or the really good families were lining up very quickly to marry an American.

It became clear to all of us at some point in the process that the best boys were never those who had left, or indeed would ever be willing to leave, India. And accordingly, the best boys would only marry the best girls—who, again and also, were those who had stayed and would never leave. It didn't really matter how tall, thin, fair, educated, attractive I was. The fatal and deadly mark against me—'she's American'—could not be compensated for. I would only be able to choose from among those sloppy seconds who themselves had left India or were looking for a way to do so.

Why would this be the case? Part of the answer, I suggest, is to be gleaned by reference to what I have termed above a more conventional conception of national identity: in particular, one that is linked to territory and geography. The answer, in this sense, resides in the question itself: if nationalism as identity is linked to territory, then it is and indeed must necessarily be the person who grew up and lives in India—regardless of their ethnic makeup—that retains, possesses, or cultivates the national identity that someone who grew up and lives outside of India has lost, relinquished, or indeed never even had or could have had. My own national identity as Indian had been compromised, even surrendered by my removal from the national soil of India and the community of Indians.

This was a personal twist on Anthony Smith's formative distinction between territorial (or civic) and ethnic nations that defies any clear and easy line between such categories. Smith argued that these constituted voluntaristic *versus* organic conceptions of national identity, respectively. The civic or territorial model of nationalism was actually a voluntaristic one (which he argued was generally more associated with western nations) in which citizenship was a matter of choice: so long as everyone belonged to some nation, it did not really matter which nation they belonged to. The ethnic or organic model, on the other hand, was a community of descent: people were born into a community or nation, and they could not choose or change their nationality (Smith 1971; 1986; 1991). Was the pre-transitional conception of Indian nationalism an ethnic or a civic one? An ethnic conception of nationalism should dictate that I was in fact Indian; but my removal from the territory of India precluded my ability to claim an Indian national identity—thus demonstrating the ways in which territory and ethnicity remained uneasily bound up with each other in a pre-transitional period.

This sense was captured by a series of full-page advertisements run in Indian newspapers and weekly newsmagazines at the beginning of 1993. In response to an initial advertisement sponsored by a group of southern California-based NRIs (non-resident Indians), a group calling itself 'Indian Citizens <u>In India</u>' (emphasis theirs)—i.e. Indians 'who Live In (Not Just Visit)' India—ran another advertisement in response, suggesting among other things that 'nine hundred thousand Indians who prefer to live in the United States [and] claim to regard as home a country they chose to desert' should be considered 'pseudo-Indians'. The advertisement suggests that it is 'presumptuous of these Indians who left "mother Bharat" and caused a severe brain drain to dictate how we Indians who remained behind should run our country' and that if NRIs 'feel strongly about India' they should 'come back and live here' (*BCAS* 1993: 68).

The political context of these volleys was the support of much of the NRI community for the forces of the Hindu right, which leftist intellectuals (and many others) in India staunchly denounced and opposed. It is beyond my purpose in this essay to do more than note, in passing, the total elision of inequality in international power structures that subsumed immigration under the facile language of preference, choice and desertion. I wish to highlight instead the strongly geographical and territorial conception of nationalism and Indian identity that underpin the statements in this advertisement. The language of 'real Indians' being those who stay and live in India, and 'pseudo-Indians' being those who leave India referred directly to the language of 'pseudo-secularism' used by the forces of the Hindu right to describe the policies of the then-dominant ruling Congress Party. The question of why diasporic Indians have leaned toward the religious right is one that research has yet to resolve. But in the early 1990s, this missive clearly conveyed a geographically and territorially bounded conception of what it means or could mean to be Indian: that is, no one who didn't live in India could or should claim to be Indian.

I have often wondered if my same personal narrative might have reached a very different set of conclusions had I been born twenty years later than I was. As it is, my story has a happy outcome—never myself entirely convinced I wanted an arranged marriage, after a few bumps in the familial road I am happily married to an American, with a son who is now himself figuring out what his own half-Indian ethnic identity might entail. In the next section, I undertake a close reading of the 2013 Bollywood blockbuster hit *YJHD* that suggests that someone like my son now not only has some place in India's imagined national community, but might virtually constitute the essence of Indian national identity in a neoliberal era.

The Celluloid: Neoliberalizing Indian National Identity in Popular Bollywood Cinema

Growing up all my life I had minimal interest in Indian (Hindi-language) films. My parents made sure we occasionally saw the 1970s blockbusters that had to be seen: *Kabhi Kabhie, Pakeezah, Amar Akbar Anthony.* When Lata Mangeshkar came to the US on tour I was delighted to have the opportunity to see her live.[6] It's not that I disliked Hindi cinema; I just wasn't very engaged with it, especially as compared to my parents' friends' children. For them, Hindi cinema was their way of affirming and performing their Indian-ness: subscribing to *Stardust* magazine,

---

[6] Widely known as the 'Nightingale' of Indian song, though now nearing the end of her career, Mangeshkar is probably the most noted female playback vocalist of the modern Indian film industry, which she dominated for no less than four decades.

keeping up with all the latest actors and gossip, learning the songs and the dances. This pop-culture way of constructing identity occasionally fooled even people who should have known better, like my parents.

It took me a longer time to find my own way to and of being Indian, of constructing my own Indian–ness. My path became academic: having found my way to the study of political science in college, I soon found my way to studying Indian politics in graduate school. I dutifully trot off to India every year or two to conduct research and renew and update my professional and cultural credentials. So my recent discovery of the pleasures of viewing Bollywood films led me to question what had changed: me or the films? Maybe some of both? As a political scientist who studies precisely these issues of identity politics, religion, gender and nationalism in India, the idea of a neoliberalized Indian national identity became most apparent to me in the context of current Bollywood films[7] as compared to prior, pre-transitional and transitional periods. In this post-transitional period, Indian national identity has moved into the world—i.e., into a global(ized) market—and made itself (or portrays itself as being) at home there. This self-relocation involves demonstrating that Indians are everywhere and can be 'at home' anywhere outside of India. But it also involves demonstrating the persisting superiority of Indian national culture even as it free-floats the globe: Indian national culture fits in anywhere, but even as it goes global it retains an internal

---

[7] Herein I focus specifically on the Hindi-language film industry, though it must be noted there are thriving film industries in most of the regional languages of India, both north and south. Whether the trends I identify here are applicable to these industries as well is still to be explored, most likely by someone with a broader range of language skills than my own.

essence that is superior to the globalized culture it now contributes to and is part of, and remains true to that essence. In this section I demonstrate these aspects through a close reading of the 2013 blockbuster Bollywood hit, *Yeh Jawaani Hai Deewani.*[8]

The globalization of the Indian film industry is widely marked as beginning with the 1995 film *Dilwale Dulhaniya Le Jayenge (DDLJ,* 'The True of Heart Will Win the Bride') (Ganti 2004; Mehta 2010; Ram 2014). This film is the story of two Indian immigrants (Raj Malhotra, played by Shah Rukh Khan and Simran Singh, played by Kajol) living in the UK who meet and fall in love with each other on a camping trip. When Simran's deeply patriarchal Indian father finds out about the romance, he whisks her back to India for an arranged marriage to a rather vile, sniveling shell of a man. Raj follows Simran back home—i.e., to India—where he ultimately wins over her whole family and finally even her father to win her hand in marriage. *DDLJ* was the first film to make an NRI a central character and let him triumph in winning the love and respect not only of Simran but also of her father and her family. In order to do so, Raj had to literally come back to India; but once he did, he was finally acknowledged to be a better man, and a better Indian, than either Simran's father or the man to whom Simran's marriage had been arranged.

The comprehensive analysis of this tectonic shift in the Indian film industry points to political-economic forces that

---

[8] As a social scientist, I feel impelled to say a word about my case selection. There are many recent films and film scenes I could analyze to demonstrate aspects of the neoliberal globalization of Indian national identity; I have chosen this one because it does so most starkly and succinctly.

buttress the shifting portrayals of Indian national identity in a cultural sense. It has been argued that the shifts represented by *DDLJ* came with the realization, or understanding, that there was a global audience for the consumption of Bollywood films. Of course, Hindi films have long been distributed and watched globally, throughout Asia and much of the Middle East. But by 1995, a more specific understanding of the Indian diaspora in the west, in particular, as a lucrative audience for Bollywood, had emerged. This required an image of India, and Indians, and Indian national identity, that was more palatable—and marketable—to Indians living and having grown up abroad and specifically in the western countries. This is what a neoliberal, globalized version of Indian national identity provided. Indeed, even the widespread use of the name Bollywood, with its obvious nod towards Hollywood as the center of the US film industry, came into play in this same time period: that is, beginning in the mid-1990s.

My analysis focuses on the Bombay film industry itself, in relation to Indian diasporas, rather than diasporic films *per se* (Desai 2004). As such, it is critical to note that the constructions I analyze are still meant for the consumption of Indian audiences in India as much as they are for the diaspora. My analysis of *YJHD* builds in important ways on Anjali Ram's (2014) superb analysis of a 2011 film, *Zindagi Na Milegi Dobara* (*ZNMD*, 'You Only Live Once'). This is the story of three boyhood friends: Imraan (played by Farhan Akhtar), Arjun (played by Hrithik Roshan), and Kabir (played by Abhay Deol), who take an adventure trip through Spain—their version of a 'bachelor party' to celebrate Kabir's engagement. The guys travel around the country, tackling various adventure sports including scuba diving, sky diving, and running with the bulls in

Pamplona. Ultimately, Kabir is persuaded to realize that the marriage he is about to undertake is not the right one for him, so he breaks off the engagement, while Arjun finds the love of his life in the free-spirited, ultimately globalized character of Laila, their scuba-diving instructor (played by Katrina Kaif). This is in many ways a modern, western narrative of 'finding yourself' free from traditional, parental, and even social boundaries. It is 'a discourse of the self that is activated through a neoliberal lens that views the marketplace...as an ideal place for self-actualization and discovery' (Ram 2014: 187). Ram also notes pertinently the gendering of these processes of self-discovery, wherein the self that is being discovered is male. The role of the women in the film is essentially relegated to being the sites on and through which the men discover themselves.

Ram's analysis of the globalized aspects of Indian national identity in this film is thorough and insightful, so I will only note a few highlights of her analysis here as it relates to my own. Ram argues that *ZNMD* imagines a space beyond the nation, where the characters represent affluent, transnational elites who travel seamlessly across national boundaries and language barriers. Hindi cinema long relied on dichotomies of east/west, good/bad, self/other, home/world, traditional/modern in which east/Indian/home/good/self/traditional always triumphed over west/world/bad/other/modern. Post-*DDLJ* films of the 1990s worked to integrate diasporic Indians back into the narrative of India, but they did so without disrupting these dichotomies: instead, they released diasporic Indians from the negative sides of them. Thus in the 1990s, diasporic Indians no longer had to be evil, corrupt, westernized, debauched; they could be good, like Raj was in *DDLJ*—though to be good they almost certainly had to come home (back to India) in some literal or figurative sense. But if they did so they could not only be good Indians, but maybe even better Indians than many resident Indians were.

ZNMD seems to have finally released all Indians—resident and diasporic alike—from any of the bonds of nationality howsoever defined, and to have finally abandoned (transcended?) these old dichotomies. In this film, Ram notes 'The nation no longer has to be anxiously ratified and the Indian self can be imagined beyond the registers of cultural essentialism' (2014: 185). Indeed, the fact that the main characters are Indian seems barely relevant to the progression of the narrative. In *ZNMD*, 'territorial definitions of identity are reconfigured and both the Indian back home and the Indian out there in the world are unified' (Ram 2014: 187). In this vision, then, it seems the nation has receded, to be replaced by a new, transglobal consumer-citizen.

The global omnipresence of Indians is explicitly established approximately midway through the film, when Imraan is searching for his biological father in Spain, but Kabir and Arjun don't yet know that he's doing so. Imran wants to drive them to his father, Salman Habib's home in Spain under the guise of searching for Habib as an artist. Having looked for Habib's work at a gallery in Barcelona at the beginning of the film, Imran explains that the woman at the gallery said Habib sells his paintings from home. The following dialogue ensues:[9]

> *Arjun*: According to the map, for Grazalema (we should take the) next right. Salman Habib. It's amazing; Indians are in every corner of the world.

---

[9] Throughout this essay, all translations from Hindi are my own.

Kabir. Really man, we're everywhere.

Ram also argues that more recent Bollywood films have now unsettled the older ties of nationalism especially as conveyed through gendered means, where women represent the nation. But rather than abandoning the nation altogether, as *ZNMD* seems to do, the nation is re-secured as a consumer nation. Where *ZNMD* goes almost as far as it seems possible to go in eliding the nation, another blockbuster hit of 2013, *YJHD*, shows us clearly how the nation is re-secured—in gendered ways—but also in fundamentally neoliberal terms: deterritorialized and individualized.

YJHD is the story of Bunny (Kabir Thapar, played by Ranbir Kapoor), a young, adventurous and talented twenty-something, a former back-row, lecture-bunking slacker who never amounted to much in school but has much grander dreams in his sights. Through a series of events, he is reunited with Naina (played by Deepika Padukone), a gorgeous but studious and bespectacled former classmate, a simple (Indian) girl who wants to live a simple (Indian) life. Throughout the movie, Naina comes to stand in for a more conventional— though updated—conception of India and all its superior values; while Bunny both seeks and represents India in/as the global beyond. The contrast between these conceptions is captured when Bunny and Naina are on a mountain-climbing ('trekking') trip[10] together and they have their first serious, intimate conversation. Bathed in moonlight on a beautiful snow-covered mountainside, Bunny opens up to Naina and shows her a scrapbook he keeps that shows all the places in the

---

[10] On the role of adventure sports in newer Bollywood films, see Ram 2014; see also Wheaton 2004.

world he wants to go.

> *Naina* (flipping pages): Venice…London…What is this
> book, Bunny?
>
> *Bunny*: My dream. I want to see every corner of the world.
>
> *Naina*: Your whole life will be gone in doing all this! When
> will you do all the rest?
>
> *Bunny*: What else is there? Studying till 22, a job at 25, a
> husband at 26, kids at 30, retirement at 60, and then?
> Waiting for death. I don't want to live any such
> ordinary life!
>
> *Naina*: So then what do you want from life, Bunny?
>
> *Bunny*: Adventure. Craziness. Every day should be so
> exciting that I can hear my heart beat in my ears. I want
> to fly, Naina. I want to run, I even want to fall. I just
> never want to stop.

Bunny's vision is the global India: unafraid and unhindered by
any fear of failure, and utterly disdainful of any simple,
traditional lifestyle, he/it wants to taste all the world has to
offer—and to give all he has to offer it. In this sense, *YJHD*,
specifically in the form of Bunny's character, represents the
same kind of unsettling of the nation that *ZNMD* does. For
Bunny, (staying) home becomes insufficient and inadequate;
India and even the world itself seem barely big enough to hold
the range and extent of his aspirations. And he does realize
them: he heads off to America on a journalism scholarship to
Northwestern University in Chicago, which becomes the
starting point for his international travels; we find him midway

through the film snapping photographs and shooting video for a travel show, courting danger—and European women—in Paris and a series of anywhere-in-Europe locales.

Were the movie to end there, it would convey a very similar conception of nationalism as *ZNMD* does. It might leave us wondering whether the nation in any discernible sense has disappeared altogether from the global, neoliberal imaginary portrayed in the film. But *YJHD* goes the next step further to show us how exactly the nation is or can be re-secured in an era of neoliberal globalization. And it does so by bringing Bunny home. The second half of the movie has Bunny return home for the wedding of a mutual friend. Naina has been in love with Bunny since their night on the mountainside; the final part of the movie revolves around how Bunny comes to realize and admit his love for Naina, and how they reconcile themselves to each other. Before this can happen, *YJHD* establishes the final, push-comes-to-shove superiority of home as India over the world and the global. Having demonstrated beyond a doubt that India can take (on) the world by giving Bunny the offer of his dream job—hosting his own travel reality show—the film sends him home to attend the wedding of a school friend, where he meets Naina again. The sense that India can both match and trump any global event is captured in the following exchange between Bunny and Naina that extends over the course of the day they spend together exploring Jaipur—notably, as tourists within their own country.

> *Naina*: So your life is like this? You must've seen lots of amazing things like this.

> *Bunny*: You can't even imagine (think), Naina. I love my life. I could never live like you people.

Naina: What do you mean, 'you people'?

Bunny: I mean, in one city, in one house, in one room, you'll spend your whole life. Doesn't the thought scare you?

Naina: Not at all. I've chosen this life. And I have no interest in living like you—like a bloody hippie.

Bunny: You're saying all this because you've never seen the world, baby! How would you know (understand) the high of living in different countries?

Naina: And how would you know what it is to stay with your own?

Bunny: You don't know what it is to sit with an unknown family and listen to their life stories.

Naina: And you don't know what it is to sit with old friends and listen to the same old stories (reminisce).

Bunny: Someday I'll take you to San Francisco and feed you my favorite mutton burgers. You'll go crazy.

Naina: Someday I'll feed you mutton *biryani*[11] made with my own hands. You'll forget your burger.

Bunny: You've never seen Paris, Naina.

Naina: Have you ever seen a child being born?

Bunny: No. But I have lots of my own kids running around Paris.

---

[11] A rice-and-meat casserole dish.

Naina: So cheap, dude!

The conversation finally becomes a perfect one-to-one, tit-for-tat exchange of one global event or experience and one corresponding Indian one.

> *Bunny*: Johannesburg, World Cup. Andres Iniesta's winning goal. [Soccer]

> *Naina*: Wankhede (Stadium). Mahendra Singh Dhoni's winning sixer! [Cricket]

> *Bunny*: California's sunshine.

> *Naina*: Mumbai's rain.

> *Bunny*: Blueberry cheesecake.

> *Naina*: Carrot halwa.

> *Bunny*: 'Phantom of the Opera' on Broadway.

> *Naina*: *DDLJ* on a single screen—with popcorn.

> *Bunny*: Actually, yeah.

On multiple occasions in the movie, Naina and Bunny acknowledge that neither one is really better than the other, but that they are just very different from each other. But after standing toe to toe with Naina, Bunny finally admits that India wins.

Here, then, are the two key characteristics of a neoliberalized national identity: deterritorialized and individualized. The nation has not gone away; it has taken different forms. Bunny represents the global, globetrotting India, entirely at home in the world—just as the characters in

ZNMD. National identity in this neoliberal form has become deterritorialized. No longer attached to the physical, geographical territory of the country, Indians and Indian-ness and thus India itself are everywhere in the world. Diasporic and mobile, Indians no longer apologize for not living or not being in India. Bunny's Indian identity is never in question throughout his globetrotting career: he apparently works for an Indian travel channel, filming and photographing with an Indian (female) host who declares herself as much of a globetrotter as he is. Bunny tells her what a thrill it is to speak Hindi in a foreign land. But it is eminently clear how entirely comfortable and successful he is and will be, wherever he is.

But Bunny's Indian-ness is entirely his own, and this comprises the second, critical aspect of a neoliberal Indian identity: delinked not only from territory, but from collective forms of identity. This is not a conventional nationalism that seeks to build a sense of collective national identity for the state. Instead of being anchored in states, collectivities or territories, it is individually anchored and manifested—and an individual choice. That is, Bunny has to choose his own Indian-ness, to be Indian and return to India. After going to the airport to leave for Paris to start his dream job, he ends up coming back to Naina and asking her to marry him. He confesses to her that she has 'trapped' him; he still wants his adventures around the globe, but he wants them hand-in-hand with her. Of course, he knows that she won't leave India. So Bunny reconciles this with the idea that there is a time for everything, and right now the time is for him to be with her. This is Bunny's own individual realization of his own individual national identity—an identity he embraces by his own individual choice, as indeed a globalized neoliberal subject can only do.

In turn, consider the Indian-ness that Naina embodies. In *YJHD* we seem to return to the well-worn trope of women embodying the nation, though I have suggested that in this film, both Bunny and Naina embody different but complementary instantiations of the nation. Naina's India is not the stuff of older representations, such as those of the 1950s and even through the 1990s. Naina is no cloying or needy, martyred India waiting and pining away for Bunny to return. She loves him, but she understands him and his need to roam. She even encourages him to go chase his dreams. When he first leaves for Chicago, she says (at 1:12:08) 'He ran after his dreams so fast he was gone in the blink of an eye…he never turned to look back…and I didn't wait for him either.' She does the same again when he returns for the wedding eight years later and realizes he loves her too. She makes it clear again that she understands him, but also that she isn't leaving her life, or India, for him. Her position is illustrated in the following exchange (at 2:13:00):

Naina: The thing is, 'I love you' is just a beginning. What happens after that?…

Bunny: We're not going to talk about this…

Naina: Bunny, I'm a simple girl. I want to live a simple life. You're not wrong, just very different than me. Please let me go.

Bunny: I can't.

Naina: So then don't go to Paris. Don't take this job that you've been dying for for years. Don't travel. Because, you know, I can't go with you. Mom, Dad, clinic, everything is here. What to do? Okay, then—you'll have to come visit me twice a year. And no fooling

around in Paris! And then after a few years you come
back here.

Bunny: Naina, I…

Naina: Ssshhh. I know you, Bunny. I understand you. I
know what your dreams are. I know what you want
from life. That's why we should forget each other. Bye.

Bunny: Don't go, Naina. This, here, feels good.

Naina: That's why I have to go.

The version of national identity that Naina represents is closer
to older conceptions in that it is more rooted in place and
community than Bunny's, as the above exchange conveys. But it
is also an independent, self-aware and self-confident
nationalism: one that will be happy with Bunny but will survive
and thrive without him as well. The women's/gender studies
scholar in me also cannot ignore the implications of how these
multiple forms of nationalism are gendered in the film. As in
ZNMD, the adventurous, globetrotting, have-it-all, free-spirited
nationalism in *YJHD* is marked as masculine—Bunny's—while
the simple life belongs to the girl, and indeed is all she really
wants though she is entirely capable of having more.

Expanding the scope of analysis to consider the interaction
between the forms of nationalism represented by these two
characters suggests what a new relationship between India and
its diaspora might entail: not the antagonistic 'real Indians' *versus*
'pseudo-Indians' discourse of the transitional and pre-
transitional periods, but rather an accepting, mutually
supporting and even mutually constitutive relation. Early in the
film, Bunny had to teach Naina how to relax, love herself and

be confident in herself and who she was. By the end of the film, Naina teaches Bunny to 'take the pleasures of where you are'. In this way, both Indias—Bunny's and Naina's—constitute India; they both have things to learn from each other and are best when they are together.

But we have also seen that in the end, Naina wins Bunny over and he does come back home. This is where nationalism reasserts itself, as indeed it always must in order to be nationalism. Perhaps the core constitutive characteristic of nationalism is that it defines itself against 'others' and must always be superior to those others. In prior eras, that superiority may have been asserted by force; in a neoliberal globalized era, it can be presented as a matter of free individual choice. Either way, to be nationalism, it has to win in the end.

I do not present this as a rose-tinged conception of national identity without significant political-economic underpinnings. As the transition proceeded, scholars have written about the pursuit—during and since the transition—by the government of India of the diasporic community: of our funds, our connections, and our loyalties. First, and to a significant still, designated by the curious (in terms of national identity) moniker NRIs, we have subsequently been designated PIOs—persons of Indian origin. If I could prove to the Indian government, with official documentation like a birth certificate or cancelled Indian passport that I was in fact born in India, or at least that my father was (apparently my mother's birth in India doesn't count the same way), then I could have unlimited rights to enter the country, purchase land, open and maintain bank accounts— almost everything but voting. The reconciliation of India with its diaspora holds significant potential gains for both: materially, and not just psychologically, though I do not have the space to unravel them here.

Conclusion: W(h)ither Nationalism?

This, then, is a glimpse of the forms that nationalism and national identity can take in a neoliberal globalized era. I have argued that in this era of neoliberal globalization, nationalism and national identity become unanchored from states, territories, and collectivities to become global, mobile, diasporic and individual identities. It is perhaps also worth delineating what this analysis does not purport to say. I do not mean to suggest that such a neoliberal (deterritorialized and individualized) nationalism is the only form in which nationalism can be found. Indeed, I have shown that more conventional conceptions of nationalism still abound and coexist with newer forms in Bollywood and through other media. As noted above, I do not intend to offer a linear or dichotomous analysis of nationalist forms; rather, I would hold that such forms in an era of neoliberal globalization must of necessity be multiple, contingent, and contested. I have sought here to analyze just a couple of the trajectories of nationalism and Indian national identity that can be identified. I hope to have demonstrated that the concept of diaspora does not entail the erasure of home—rather it redirects where and how we must find it, or construct it.

In general, neoliberalism has come in for critical analysis for its unleashing of inequality and withdrawing of any forms of institutional support for those—people, countries, and otherwise—at the bottom end of the spectrum, in the name of individual freedom. But the problems with neoliberalism do not suggest that its predecessors were necessarily better—more equitable or more productive of justice, however conceived—than neoliberalism itself is proving to be. Similarly with nationalism, it is difficult to argue that conventional forms of nationalism have been better or worse in these senses than a more neoliberalized form identified herein. Is neoliberalized nationalism more or less likely to be associated with war and conflict? Ethnic hatreds and religious fundamentalisms? Or, we may be left to ask, if not these, then with what injustices of its own might a neoliberal nationalism (come to) be associated?

Nationalism and national identity have been and remain notoriously difficult to capture, define, and study. Nationalism is among the most analytically elusive and politically relevant of phenomena: studied across disciplines and deployed in limitless manifestations, it is as important as it is difficult to understand nationalism and national identity. I have studied and researched nationalism—specifically Indian nationalism—through historical, political, sociological and even legal lenses. As much as an academic and intellectual exercise, the attempt to study and understand nationalism and national identity is also deeply personal. This essay represents, for me, two new ways to try to grasp this elusive form of identity: through auto-ethnography and film analysis. I present the analysis not as final or definitive, but as potential new tools in a vast toolkit necessary to begin to unravel and understand the permutations and manifestations of nationalism and national identity in an era of neoliberal globalization. For whatever forms globalization takes going forward, it seems it would behoove scholars not to write off nationalism anytime soon, but to look instead for what forms and shapes it might reappear in.

References

Anderson, Benedict. 1983. *Imagined communities: Reflections on the origin and spread of nationalism.* London: Verso.

Appadurai, Arjun. 1996. *Modernity at large: Cultural dimensions of globalization.* MN: University of Minnesota Press.

Bardhan, Pranab K. 2010. *Awakening giants, feet of clay: Assessing the economic rise of China and India.* NJ: Princeton University Press.

BCAS. 1993. *Bulletin of Concerned Asian Scholars.* Special issue: Women and religious nationalism in India. 25 (4) (Oct.-Dec.).

Chakravarty, Sumita S. 1993. *National identity in Indian popular cinema, 1947-1987.* TX: University of Texas Press.

de Casanova, Erynn Masi, and Afshan Jafar, eds. 2013. *Bodies without borders.* NY: Palgrave Macmillan.

Desai, Jigna. 2004. *Beyond Bollywood: The cultural politics of South Asian diasporic film.* NY: Routledge.

Ganti, Tejaswini. 2004. *Bollywood: A guidebook to popular Hindi cinema.* NY: Routledge.

Gellner, Ernest. 1983. *Nations and nationalism.* NY: Cornell University Press.

Harvey, David. 2005. *A brief history of neoliberalism.* NY: Oxford University Press.

Horowitz, Donald L. 2000. *Ethnic groups in conflict.* CA:

University of California Press.

Jafar, Afshan, and Erynn Masi de Casanova, eds. 2013. *Global beauty, local bodies*. NY: Palgrave Macmillan.

Khilnani, Sunil. 1999. *The idea of India*. NY: Farrar Straus Giroux.

Lechner, Frank J., and John Boli, eds. 2012. *The globalization reader*. 4th ed. MA: J. Wiley & Sons.

Mehta, Rini Bhattacharya, and Rajeshwari Pandharipande, eds. 2010. *Bollywood and globalization: Indian popular cinema, nation, and diaspora*. NY: Anthem Press.

Nayar, Baldev Raj. 2014. *Globalization and India's economic integration*. Washington, DC: Georgetown University Press.

Ohmae, Kenichi. 1995. *The end of the nation state: The rise of regional economies*. NY: Free Press.

Ram, Anjali. 2014. *Consuming Bollywood: Gender, globalization, and media in the Indian diaspora*. NY: Peter Lang.

Roy, Srirupa. 2007. *Beyond belief: India and the politics of postcolonial nationalism*. NC: Duke University Press.

Sachs, Jeffrey, Ashutosh Varshney, and Nirupam Bajpai. 2000. *India in the era of economic reforms*. New Delhi: Oxford University Press.

Smith, Anthony D. 1991. *National identity*. NV: University of Nevada Press.

———. 1986. *The ethnic origins of nations*. NY: Basil Blackwell.

———. 1971. *Theories of nationalism*. London: Duckworth.

Steger, Manfred B., and Ravi K. Roy. 2010. *Neoliberalism: A very short introduction.* NY: Oxford University Press.

Strange, Susan. 1996. *The retreat of the state: The diffusion of power in the world economy.* NY: Cambridge University Press.

Turner, Bryan S., ed. 2010. *The Routledge international handbook of globalization studies.* NY: Routledge.

von Schnitzler, Antina. 2008. Neoliberalism. In *International encyclopedia of the social sciences,* ed. William A. Darity. 2nd ed., 473-5. MI: Macmillan Reference USA.

Wheaton, Belinda. 2004. *Understanding lifestyle sports: Consumption, identity, and difference.* NY: Routledge.

4

~~~~~~

Imagining the Present and (re)presenting the Imaginary: Belonging and dejection among the Irish community in Belgium

SEAN O DUBHGHAILL

The recent turn in the social sciences, which emphasises the role played by the social and cultural imaginary (Taylor, 2004; Salazar and Graburn, 2014), presents an interesting lens through which the concept of diaspora can be (re)imagined. Taking the imaginary as our jumping off point we can ask long-standing questions anew; imaginaries, therefore, can help us inform the manner through which Diasporic groups imagine 'home', mobilities, sameness and otherness, community, the past as well as their possible future(s).

If we adhere to Anderson's (1983) maxim that communities are imagined entities, diasporic communities are, in a sense, doubly-imagined, given that they are not at home, but a sense of commonality still remains. How sameness and difference are imagined among the Irish diaspora seems to depend largely upon the extent of engagement with the host country. Examining the Irish in Belgium, then, is an excellent case study to this end, given the language barriers as well as the interrelated history the two countries share. The shared history informs the diaspora's imaginary in two ways, both the older history which extends back as far as 1607, when Franciscan migrants were housed in Belgium's historic University in Louvain, as well as more recent history when Ireland joined the European Union, whose major institutions are located in Brussels, in 1973.

This work examines how members of the global Irish community (thought to be 80 million-strong worldwide) recapitulate a sense of belonging in Belgium by reproducing or simulating products of national belonging and identity (music, sports and social life in particular). The work then traces instances in which efforts were made to imagine an Irishness which was then narrativised and intersubjectively authenticated-to varying degrees of success.

Imagining home in the present and being present at home:

There is a particular vignette, from my own childhood, which might serve as the connective tissue between an examination of the literature on the Irish community, and how both of those terms might be understood anthropologically, and how the methodology most apposite to their examination might be framed. I believe that this can be concisely conveyed by reflecting back on formative experiences from my childhood which took place in the company of my Irish-American cousins; believing with Robin Boylorn and Mark Orbe (2014) that auto-ethnography can be used to convey information derived from sense experience and Peter Collins and Anselma Gallinat (2010) who claim that the self is the primary conveyance of that recounting these events can serve to heighten the experience of ethnographic engagement, rather than detracting from them.

In March of 1993 my Irish-American mother drove myself and two of Irish-American cousins down to a remote castle in County Cork, in the province of Munster in Ireland. At the very top of Blarney castle, which is surrounded by lush groves of beautifully-arranged thickets and meadows, is a kind of enclosure which is surrounded by fortress walls but which is also exposed to the elements. The main attraction lies off to one side, and atop a small pile of scaffolding. The Blarney stone, which when kissed is thought to imbue those undergoing the ritual with the gift of 'eloquence', is the reason we have arrived. First, it might be important to stress that while the gift which is thought to be obtained through this odd ritual is not exactly eloquence as such but is, in actuality, commonly referred to as the gift of the gab, a metonymical construction which brings together those undergoing the ritual and those living in Ireland. It is, without reading between the lines, thought to involve the initiand's induction into receiving the gift of being seamlessly akin to the Irish in manners of speech.

This highly prized ethnic marker was why we were here and my cousins ran quickly past our tour guide in order to ensure that they had a good place in line. I was more fearful and hesitant. What was required, as can be seen partially in fig 1., is that the neophyte is required to lie on their back, grab a hold of two iron bars which are necessary to secure oneself and to kiss a part of the rock which is smoother than elsewhere on the castle's inner wall. An attendant assists in this, laying his hands on the torso of anyone supplicating themselves to the rite. What cannot be observed in fig 1, though, is that there is a sheer drop, protected only by a fine grill, where the head of the prospective initiate would lie. I am quite sure, thinking back upon it, that my imagination has pronounced the fineness of the grill and if I were to see it now I believe that it would be more than adequate, but there was no convincing me of that at that time. My fear of heights had gotten the better of me and I stood ramrod still as my cousins beckoned me to join them in the queue. I saw participant after participant undergo the procedure, I remember the majority of them being (Irish-)Americans who had Irish roots, but no matter how expertly it was conducted, time after time, I could not be convinced to partake.

I remember feeling quite embarrassed at this. My cousins returned and were now affecting Irish accents. My mother spoke to me shortly thereafter, upon seeing my dejection. "You know that you don't have to kiss the Blarney stone though, right?" I was intrigued. "Why not?" "Well, you were born here, your father is Irish and you speak Irish. There's no need for you to do this like there is for them. You already are Irish." I remember feeling incredibly relieved.

What is at stake in this vignette is still as relevant to my research today as it was when it occurred over two decades ago. In unpacking what happened, or at least how I remember what had happened, what was at stake was the concretising of a claim to belonging by way of something metonymically, irreducibly associated with one's identity; my cousins had travelled from overseas and in so doing had been given the opportunity to (re)connect with their roots. To me, we had driven for about three hours to a new locale. What was more was that I didn't have to get in touch with a connection which was imaginary in nature; my connection seems to have been secured by a kind of factual bind and just by dint of what might be viewed as contingent things, I was thought to be exempt from having to commemorate my identity. What follows is an examination of

Figure 1: Kissing the Blarney Stone, Image in the public domain.

recent work on imaginaries and which takes community to be its focal point. This emerged as a necessary topic of study due in part to experiences similar to those highlighted above; namely, the necessity to commemorate an identity which is not affirmed or imagined to exist in the context of a community.

Imagining Community.

Believing, with Anderson (1983), that communities which are imagined and depend largely upon subjects who can, by definition, never be present or fully represented we must understand that imagination functions in a manner that can create a 'we-feeling' around remote or proximal fellow-subjects:

> It is *imagined* because the members of even the smallest nation will never know most of their fellow-members, meet them, or even hear of them, yet in the minds of each lives the image of their communion. (Anderson, 1983:6. Emphasis in Original)

The notion of community appears, in the beginning of the 20th century, to be part of a dualistic whole which relates, for the purposes of the-then popular exposition of the inner workings of structural functionalism, the individual and community (or to the more utilitarian construct of group). Raymond Williams' account is one which attempts to disembed the term community from its utilitarian capacity, instead displaying the warmth with which the concept has been embraced and the homogeneity that the term itself presupposes:

> Community can be the warmly persuasive word to describe an existing set of relationships, or the warmly persuasive word to describe an alternative set of relationships. What is most important, perhaps, is that

unlike all other terms of social organization (state, nation, society, etc.) it seems never to be used unfavourably, and never to be given any positive opposing or distinguishing term. (Williams, 1985:76)

Community, from among any of the terms used to characterise or map out various models of territorially-defined intersubjectivity, describes both a state of existing relationships but also points to the emergence of new sets of relationships. What might stand in opposition to community, at the ontological level, may be something akin to the tenacious purchase over the agglomeration of cultural difference to which it lays claim. This is examined in Bauman (2000) who takes as his point of departure Williams' contention that community's primary feature, apart from its pliability, is its abiding quality:

> In so far as they need to be defended to survive and they need to appeal to their own members to secure that survival by their individual choices and take for that survival individual responsibility - all communities are postulated; projects rather than realities, something that comes after, not before the individual choice. The community 'as seen in communitarian paintings' would be tangible enough to be invisible and to afford silence; but then communitarians won't paint its likenesses, let alone exhibit them. (Bauman, 2000:169)

In the example provided at the outset of this work, then, what appears to have occurred is the bringing into alignment of a community's commemorative sense of itself and the outsider perspective thereupon. Community's abiding quality, as well as the parenthetical difficulties involved in its invocation, is also a topic tackled in Vered Amit & Nigel Rapport's *The Trouble with*

Community: Anthropological Reflections on Movement, Identity and Collectivity (2002). Community is put forward in the work, in a manner similar to Bauman, as being a tentative entity which has a postulated quality but is one which is more useful as a collective designation than it is as an individually-felt entity. In Amit's closing remarks she writes that:

> Over the last three decades, cultural analysts have increasingly resorted to this form of proclaimed category (i.e. Community, Ed.), fictive communality as the theoretical model for all forms of community. But some of the most crucial forms of fellowship, of belonging, are barely marked by explicit symbolic icons... But some of the personal links that arise through these experiences carry on. Most people are able to transform some of these encounters into more dyadic personal relationships that can be exported into different contexts. (Amit & Rapport, 2002:63-64)

The enduring quality community is thought to express, even after having left one supposed community to live in another, is the express interest of the present work as well as the examination of the 'exportability' and transformative components of an expression of identity that one group is thought to possess and to undergo. What is overlooked, though, and which is very often encountered in the field is the rejection of particular commemorative acts made by members of the Irish community abroad and on the grounds of ethnic affiliation.

Community, thought of in exactly this manner, is merely a reflection of ethnicity which is coupled with a presupposed, imaginatively proscribed quality which unites those it is thought to encapsulate:

> [C]ommunal, local, regional, national, and 'racial' identities can all be understood as locally and historically specific variants on a general and ancient theme of collective identification: ethnicity. Each of these variants says something about "the social organisation of culture difference"… They are, if you like, culturally imagined and socially consequential. (Jenkins, 2002:125)

The manner in which the composition of communities, as having a perceived similarity, is similar in kind to that articulated by William Shakespeare in *Henry V* (1599) in that the necessity for interlocutors to presuppose the possibility of similarity is the grounds for a common Irishness at all:

> "………………But pardon, Gentles all:
> The flat unraysed spirits, that hath dar'd
> On this unworthy Scaffold, to bring forth
> So great an Object. Can this Cock-Pit hold
> The Vastie fields of France? Or can we cramme
> Within this Wooden O, the very Caskes
> That did affright the Ayre of Agincourt?" (Henry V, Lines 8-14)

The possibilities for Irishness to be expressed in its entirety will, out of necessity, be one which is imagined into existence, is supplemental in nature and is geographically unbound.

This mode of belonging is also interpellated, in the manner prescribed in Althusser (1971), an excellent example of which is the observation of the manner through which a community, imagined to exist in one way, can change its pre-ideological ethnic construction of itself. This is achieved in Noel Ignatiev's *How the Irish became white* (1995) in which, only in the work's afterword it must be noted, the author reveals that the work does not concern race at all but, instead, focuses on ethnicity and ethnic transformation:

> In Britain, the Irish constituted a subject race. Because blackness was the badge of the slave in America, people from Ireland who went there entered the free labour system, which made them part of the dominant race. As unskilled workers, they occupied the lowest place within it. Ethnicity marked the spot. (Ignatiev, 1995:186.)

Curiously placed in the postscript, this final section reveals the point of departure of the book which concerns the manner in which it was possible for the Irish (not members of discrete communities or from particular locales, but to whom the label was thought to indiscriminately apply) to belong in the United States over time.

The necessity of belonging though is contingent upon imagined similarities which are borne out of time-tested interactions within communities, however tentatively they have been conceptualised of. Recent work, which takes the ancestral components of roots and belonging as critical objects, have drawn some attention in anthropological circles, not least the figures of Deleuze and Guattari. In order to treat the root, and the root-metaphor of the nation state as being suspect, we might investigate the possibility, at all, of having an ancestral, secure metaphysical and fixed ground in which to embed these claims. Quentin Meillasoux, son of Africanist anthropologist Claude Meillasoux, has examined exactly this by applying new metaphors of fossils proper and what he calls arche-fossils which bespeak a time period prior to the emergence of subjective thought; what this indicates is that statements made by subjects who arrive on the scene of existence, and which precedes the appearance of the arche-fossil, are impossible- or at least extremely problematic. His formulation and the parenthetical question of what to make of ancestral statements is as follows:

> A fossil is a material bearing traces of pre-historic life: but what I call an arche-fossil is a material indicating traces of "ancestral" phenomena anterior even to the emergence of life. I call "ancestral" a reality- a thing or event- which existed before life on earth... So my question is very straightforward: What are the conditions of possibility of ancestral statements? (Meillasoux, 2008:15)

If we fully subscribe to Meillasoux's position what emerges, in effect, is the revelation that statements of any kind, whether they relate to community, ethnicity or to what comprises an ancestral pedigree are all of an imaginary sort. What's more though, as we turn to an examination of broader trends in examinations of imaginaries is that they relate to more than simply claims of belonging and conditions the manner in which that belonging can be critiqued. The section which follows examines the discrepancy concerning the composition of the Irish diaspora in figures which also underscores the role played by imaginaries in belonging.

The Irish Community in Belgium in figures and imaginaries:

According to the latest Statbel estimates (as of 1/1/2012) the entire Irish expatriate community in Belgium comprises 3,336 individuals, the majority of which occupy the 18-64 years old age bracket. Other estimates go as high as 10,000 for the turn of the century (Harvey, 1999). A higher figure still is often circulated among the Eurocrats working in the Irish Permanent representation to the European Union and the figure 15,000 is believed to be an accurate estimate which extrapolates upon Harvey's figure.[1]

Bronwen et al's study (2002) *A study of the existing sources of information and analysis about Irish emigrants and Irish communities abroad* is illuminating for a different reason, which is that of the 20 page list of citations and references only 4 of which concern the Irish diaspora in, what is termed, the "Rest of EU". The migrant profile in the aforementioned study is drawn in the following manner:

> Although there have been close connections between Ireland and European countries other than Britain for centuries, migration for employment on a significant scale is a very recent phenomenon. It belongs clearly to the latest economic phase of emigration, that of global mobility, and is in striking contrast to the social model of movement 'from the known to the known' (Bronwen et al., 2002.)

---

[1] This was the explanation I was given when looking for figures in an earlier stage of research and I was invited to submit a more accurate number of Irish Emigrants if I ever came across it.

The conclusion that can be drawn, therefore, is that large imaginary networks are in effect by which movement from the 'home' land to another (Anglophone historically) context is possible after the imaginary of the place has been successfully transmitted.

What can be observed immediately is the Anglophone preference in migration over multilingual migration. The figure postulated here for those individuals in Belgium who identify themselves as Irish, or possibly as having a special affinity with the people of Ireland, is estimated to be 400,000. This figure, as we have observed, far exceeds any currently on record but that does not make it a false one. The Irish diaspora cannot be thought of in terms of strictly delineated patterns of continuity and which would be extremely difficult if not impossible to do given their internal differences (see, Doyle, 1999). Instead, we might extrapolate that the diaspora, in having an effect on the region in which they reside, change the subjective orientations of those they encounter as well as undergoing change themselves. Instead of capitulating this alteration in the composition of the diaspora as something which is to its detriment, i.e. that it is losing something integral to itself, we are reminded in Hall (1990) that this is a necessary component of those elements of exposure to other cultures which lead to identities being reconstructed anew:

> The diaspora experience as I intend it here is defined, not by essence or purity, but by the recognition of a necessary heterogeneity and diversity; by a conception of 'identity' which lives with and through, not despite, difference; by *hybridity*. Diaspora identities are those which are constantly producing and reproducing

themselves anew, through transformation and difference.
(Hall, 1990: 235, emphasis in original)

What might be missing from an examination of this kind
though is the experience of the diaspora and other
hibernophiles who encounter those people who believe their
connection comprises more than just an imaginary one and
believe that members of the diaspora cannot imagine a present
and rely on a co-opting of the past, a topic to which I wish to
turn next.

The act of dissociation, that can occur within the context
of home by alien spectators attempting to commodify aspects
of Irish life as it is lived, is exemplified in Quinn (2001) who
analyses the manner in which 'traditional' crafts become
transformed into palatable tourist fare. Quinn details her
ethnographic experience among a small group of interested
Irish speakers (an Tapéis gael or Irish tapestry) who are
attempting to revive the craft of weaving as part of their
purported heritage. The ethnographer details the manner in
which in anticipation of an upcoming event a 'frontstage',
intended for consumption by the tourist gaze, is erected which
bears little commonality with the group's everyday workings and
tasks. This presentification of cultural heritage, as though it
were contemporaneous and in keeping with life in the present
age, causes proponents to become alienated from their own
attempts to revive the lost heritage and induces, in one
informant, the desire to emigrate and to start anew. In closing,
Quinn writes:

[T]he reconfiguring of persons who seek to define
themselves as cultural artefacts, and who subsequently
become defined as such, means that they as well as the

objects they create are susceptible of coming under the influence and power of continuing objective discourses...To colonizer, church and state in Ireland is now added tourist, the newest representer who, because s/he is solicited and approached, arrives with even more disingenuous acerbity. (Quinn, 2001:38)

The consumption of Irish-themed fare, though, is not simply done by tourists who arrive with the express intention of watching, while simultaneously objectifying the display, is thought to be most rife among third and fourth generation Irish-American for whom St. Patrick's day is the single largest conveyance through which a collective assembly can join together and express pride in their identity. This includes both the Irish and the non-Irish and is thought to imbue those in the audience with a kind of provisional and temporal license over Irishness[2]. This is oftentimes difficult given that their identity has been formed, not by having been born in Ireland, but has been mediated through simulations and other representations of that identity:

> The negotiations of such Irish Americans' relationship to Ireland becomes one dominated by the concept of a home nation which is not only elsewhere, but which is not directly and personally remembered. It is this moment at which Ireland becomes, for the majority of the world's population who identify themselves as Irish, a home understood through the consumption of narrativised images- principally those of film and

---

[2] For a comprehensive history of St. Patrick's Day festivities, which are documented in largely Anglophone communities, see Cronin and Adair (2002).

tourism- rather than first-hand memory or experience. (Rains, 2006:141)

For some, this lack of first-hand knowledge is something of a stumbling block, with respect to inter-ethnic acknowledgment. What this means is that those who do not live in the present at one location can only live through it with respect to its goneness, through commemoration. This topic is discussed below with respect to the works of Walter Benjamin and Pierre Nora.

Relocating the Irish diaspora in place:

The Irish diaspora is a term employed to refer to the Irish community abroad by the Irish government[3] and by those who identify as Irish-American or for others who long for 'home' in other ways, as well as the people of Ireland themselves, have undergone tremendous changes over the past forty years and academics have begun to pay more attention to changes over time than to the continuity which presents itself between shifts in historical epochs. This continuity is guaranteed by a solidarity expressed through the imagination:

> [Diasporas] are formed by the forcible or voluntary dispersion of peoples to a number of countries. They constitute a diaspora if they continue to evince a common concern for their 'homeland' (sometimes an imagined homeland) and come to share a common fate with their own people, wherever they happen to be. (Cohen & Kennedy, 2000:32)

---

[3] This is discussed with respect to "The Gathering" the most recent attempt by the Irish government to bring a population, who imagine themselves to be Irish, into existence while inviting them to return to Ireland in the year 2013.

However, this belief in a shared common fate is neither something given nor is it something immune to, or remote from, greater processes of change which the diaspora can undergo, a concern evident and examined below with respect to the works of Deleuze and Guattari (1986) and Mclean (2004).

The notion of the 'Irish diaspora' is one of a recent composition, rather than referring to them as an Irish community abroad in the strictest sense, whose complexities have been examined previously, and which burst onto the scene and into the popular lexicon after a speech given by former President of Ireland Mary Robinson in 1998. Robinson highlighted the work of Eavan Boland, which had been written a decade previously, concerning the treatment of members of the diaspora by those who remained at home:

> Like oil lamps we put them out the back,
> of our houses, of our minds. We had lights
> better than, newer than and then
> a time came, this time and now
> we need them. (Boland, 2012)

Robinson attempted to redirect attention to the swathe of Irish people abroad who had been consigned to elsewhere from the national consciousness and is thought to have been the driving force behind more attention being paid to the Irish diaspora.

This became enshrined in law only that same year because article two of the Irish Constitution had to be rewritten in light of the "Good Friday agreement"; the original iteration reads simply: "The national territory consists of the whole island of Ireland, its islands and the territorial seas". The primacy of the territory in the composition of the citizen is concisely stated and is such that the diaspora can no longer identify closely with a citizenry, the limits of belonging of which do not extend overseas. This was changed in 1998 to acknowledge the special relationship that Ireland has with its overseas diaspora and currently reads:

> It is the entitlement and birthright of every person born in the island of Ireland, which includes its islands and seas, to be part of the Irish Nation. That is also the entitlement of all persons otherwise qualified in accordance with law to be citizens of Ireland. Furthermore, the Irish nation cherishes its special affinity with people of Irish ancestry living abroad who share its cultural identity and heritage." (Articles 2 and 3 of the Irish Constitution, 2002)

The concept of diaspora, as it applies to the manner in which the Irish government has instrumentalised the diaspora and how their special affinity, which might be framed as a 'we-consciousness', stems from inter-ethnic acknowledgment. However, in the gradated acknowledgment of citizens versus denizens we might observe that there remains a central identity which exogenously cherishes those who are, and remain, outside of Ireland.[4]

Differentiation between the homeland-dwelling, immobile citizens of Ireland and the diasporic, migrant population is a matter for concern here for anthropologists. To address the manner in which the Irish community abroad encounter their fellow Europeans in situ and to ground this

---

[4] This has led to an imaginary line being drawn and maintained in various discourses between 'real' and 'fake' or 'plastic' Irish people. I have examined this elsewhere (O' Dubhghaill, 2014).

question, such that it can be assessed and examined, the population, among whom this question was put to, were members of the Irish community in Belgium. There is not much written on the topic of Irish migrants to Belgium in the 21st century and the reason for that may be quite simple to explain, Belgium's propinquity to Ireland; in other words, their closeness to one another (and their parenthetically assumed similarity to one another) has failed to capture the interest of many scholars[5]. Cronin (2008) writes:

> The permanent move to Canada but not the sojourn to Sicily, the emigrants' letters home from Australia, but not the visit to Berlin, become objects of critical inquiry. Irrevocability risks becoming a talisman of authenticity (real travel [exile] v. superficial travel [tourism]) and concentration on the Irish in New Communities may narrow the world to encounters with varieties of Anglophone Irishness and neglect individual Irish experiences of a multi-lingual and multicultural planet. (Cronin, 2008)

Examining this particular community in Europe, therefore, is intended to occupy both the lacunae which stems from the tendency to examine the Irish community abroad in Anglophone countries solely, as identified by Cronin, and to re-'people' discourses conventionally occupied by political scientists.

---

[5] Another possibility is the idea that Ireland is somehow close to continental Europe is one which is only thinkable recently and in the context of Ireland's accession to Europe in 1973.

Imaginaries in Review:

To begin it might be necessary to disembed the exclusively narrativised or mental character of imaginaries. Imaginaries, for instance, can be co-extensive with bodily attitudes. This is the manner in which Mauss discusses this process with respect to the imaginary of the act of digging and how it is realised, and brought into a new practical relation, in other contexts. Mauss writes in 'Technique de la corps':

> "The English troops I was with did not know how to use French spades, which forced us to change 8,000 spades a division when we relieved a French division, and vice versa. This plainly shows that a manual knack can be learnt only slowly. Every technique properly so called has its own form. But the same is true of every attitude of the body. Each society has its own special habits." (Mauss, 1973:73).

This is not to say, as Mauss warns, that imaginaries can't come to be shared or co-occupied; the process is a slow but possible horizon of engagement. Imaginaries can also comprise more than a belonging which is somehow remote or factual, such as in the vignette involving my Irish-American cousins, but as something dormant which can be tapped into, such as examined in Leite who traces the manner in which 'roots tourists' encounter their Jewish-Portuguese ancestor's experience of suffering in *judiaria* and who restates that travelling can incur the re-experiencing of what is past in what is presented:

> Some visitors engage in what I term *imaginative reconstruction*, not merely sensing the past or reliving ancestral experience in the present, but actually imagining themselves "there, then." This "as if" mode of

experiential commemoration can produce powerful emotional effects. (Leite, 2005:290)

Moreover, and for the purposes of the present work, imaginaries are also the predicates of memory given that the past is so constantly under threat of being forgotten. It is this topic to which the following section turns, with respect to the work of Nora (1989)

Nora (1989) contends that it is out of the concern for something, which is becoming jeopardised, that we attempt to memorialise it. He writes:

> There are lieux de mémoire, sites of memory, because there are no longer milleu de mémoire, real environments…the process that is carrying us forward and our representations of that process are of the same kind. If we were able to live within memory, we would not have needed to consecrate lieux de mémoire in its name. (Nora, 1989:7-8)

The fact that our memory isn't immediately accessible might mean that in order to commemorate something at all we should have to acknowledge its having occurred by way of a memorial. Collections of national symbols can come to be assembled and concretised in places in a manner reminiscent of the rules of accumulation, described above, and the acts of not-forgetting the sum total of the representations, which have become objectified, becomes central to its preservation and continued acknowledgment.

Just as there are imagined communities, in the sense outlined in Anderson (1983), so too can we contend that sites in which memories have been aggregated and construed are maintained in a manner which is artificial. They are artificially constructed, literally and post facto, and their intention is to withstand as a lasting memory which derives from a community desiring that that be so and as a kind of active consciousness. Nora contends that it is this operation which allows collective memory to come into existence but which also exposes it to danger:

> We buttress our identities upon such bastions, but if what they defended were not threatened, there would be no need to build them. (Ibid, 12)

These bastions become the point of departure for the grand project of nationalism in which the memorialisation of the past provides the grounds for legitimating the situations in which people find themselves in the present. The past, as imagined collectively and selectively, comes to occupy the role conventionally played by origin myths which are now tasked with the project of imagining a 'we-consciousness'. As Nora writes:

> It is no longer genesis that we seek but instead the decipherment of what we are in the light of what we are no longer (Ibid, 18)

The past becomes a jumping off point rather than the exact point at which origin myths root themselves. The idea that the past allows for a place to have an identity is what is put across by Nora, but it is sufficient here only to note that it is precisely because the past is vulnerable, to revisionism or to forgetting, that the manner in which people relate to their Irishness is vulnerable too. This vulnerability may ignite the desire to ensure that imposters do not co-opt the authenticity and sacredness of memory. This is a lamentation of a similar sort to that alluded to above, namely that were we able to live within memory or live through place we would not need to designate it linguistically, post-factually or otherwise.

This invariably leads to conversations about authenticity which bring into clear contradistinction the harsh lines of authentication which separate 'true' Irish person from imagined claims-maker. Given that Benjamin claims that "[T]he presence of the original is the prerequisite to the concept of authenticity" (Benjamin, [1955] 1999; 214) we can analyse the distance from a given place as being sufficient conditions for claims of any individual's 'inauthenticity' to be made. Benjamin speaks directly to this concern:

> The authenticity of a thing is the essence of all that is transmissible from its beginning, ranging from its substantive duration to its testimony to the history which it has experienced. Since the historical testimony rests on the authenticity, the former, too, is jeopardized by reproduction when substantive duration ceases to matter. (Ibid: 215)

The problem with Benjamin's sentiment, and if we concur with Meillasoux, is that we have to acknowledge that place reconstitutes itself over time and so there's never one place to which to return. Deleuze and Guattari (1986, 1988) instead of a having a metaphysics which is grounded, argue for the necessity of acknowledging the multiplicity of the contingencies of time and place and the claims thereto:

> Make Rhizomes, not roots, never plant! Don't sow, grow offshoots! Don't be one or multiple, be multiplicities!

Run lines, never plot a point!... *Between* things does not designate a localizable relation going from one thing to the other and back again, but a perpendicular direction, a transversal movement that sweeps one *and* the other away, a stream without beginning or end that undermines its banks and picks up speed in the middle. (Deleuze and Guattari, 1988:27-28. Emphasis in Original.)

While traditions are narrativised, usually-singular, invented phenomenon, the maintenance of a feeling of continuity has tended to take the official dictum of the nation-state as its primary port of call instead of, as Deleuze and Guattari contend, along bizarre, tangential and multiplex webs of belongings and identities. The reason for this singular necessity, according to Mclean, appears to reside in the nation-state's desire to represent itself reiteratively:

The archival rehabilitation of an ostensibly lost world reveals the state's cultural self-legitimation to be analogous to a feat of necromancy, seeking to transmute the vestiges of a foregone past into a redemptive vision of national persistence and renewal... It is not enough for the nation-state simply to assert the antiquity of its ancestral pedigree; for its claims to be culturally persuasive, it is necessary that these imputed primordial beginnings be reiteratively summoned and deployed in the present. (Mclean, 2004:29)

Another demonstration for the possible undesirability for aligning oneself, by way of the imaginary to a particular community, is the distinction drawn between nativity and indigeneity. Niezen writes, in quite a long but powerful passage:

Indigenous identities are largely built on the foundations of victimization and grievance, invoked through both collective memory and daily experience. Tracing these identities to their sources, we find that those who call themselves indigenous peoples are at the same time those most commonly the targets of untrammelled ethnic and racial hatred, dispossessed of lands and livelihoods through coercion, impoverished by exclusion from formal economies and deprived, by virtue of their "distinct" status, of the rights and benefits of citizenship within states. Their suffering and the collective identities that derive from it come largely from a tendency on the part of states and corporations to remove them to practice their own subsistence methods and other dimensions of culture, and then to deny them new economic opportunities by invoking, directly or indirectly, their attachment to "traditional" practices. (Niezen, 2003:221)

So, while connections which are imagined are conditioned from within by desirability and patterns of consumption they are also conditioned from without by counterclaims and the outright rejection of belonging, a topic to which the section which follows is devoted.

"He's not Irish. He's not. Just listen to him": When imagination is not enough:

One occasion on which the grounds for qualifying someone as being 'properly' or 'improperly' Irish occurred around in February, 2014 in Leuven, Belgium. I was fortunate enough on one occasion to bear witness to this process as it unfolded. I was sitting outside of a pub, at which an Irish person worked but which is not generally thought to be Irish, and after I had finished speaking over the phone to a friend in English a stranger tried to spark up a conversation. He had a strong Australian lilt in his accent and began telling me about his girlfriend for whom he was waiting. He then moved on to the topic of my accent and wanted to know, specifically, where I hailed from in Ireland and I obliged. He then told me, proudly, that he was also from Dublin having been born in the Coombe Hospital. As he relayed this story, though, the Irish employee came over, removed some glasses, and proceeded to disagree. He looked at me: "He's not Irish. He's not. Just listen to him." I was caught slightly off guard and my conversation partner had suddenly become sullen and dejected. I remained silent for a moment; "We're always joking like that", he eventually responded in a hushed voice. A feeling of dejection was palpable and I had also, during my fieldwork stay, been privy to some efforts which are taken, which fly below the radar of fully passing oneself of as Irish, which include the self-designation of 'hibernophile' rather than entertaining 'false' notions of Irishness. A possible reason for this frank dismissal, which resulted in a kind of sorry dejection, is the perceived feeling on the part of the bar man that Irishness is a commodity in low-supply, similar to Quinn's (2001) informants, and who feel it to somehow be in jeopardy.

A variation of this theme can be found elsewhere. Another informant, Emma, and I chatted about life in Leuven often. She expressed an interest in the research question and we exchanged numbers. We met a number of times over the two months which followed during which time we were able to get to know one another. I became familiar with the eclectic group of Erasmus students with whom she spent time and we both attended football and rugby matches in Stapletons, and Irish pub in Leuven, at her invitation. We casually chatted during which time I made mention of a Primark (a popular clothes retailer in Ireland and elsewhere) situated in Liege and she mentioned that she had been looking for an excuse to travel to Liege and we made an arrangement to travel out that Sunday.

While the trip itself was enjoyable, but unremarkable, we spoke about upcoming prospects, her love-life and the quality of Liege's landmarks but it was the return journey's conversation that really stood out. We had boarded the wrong train bound for Leuven (an ICE train- an intercity train rather than an inter-regional IC train) and after being scolded by the ticket inspector our topic turned to the basic components of Irishness. Seated in the interstices of the carriages on either side Emma began to outline a wide permutation of situations, each of which concluded with the question of whether what she had outlined would qualify the fictive person she had outlined as being Irish. It began with questions of parentage; "say someone's mam is Irish but their dad is from somewhere else but they live in Ireland- does that make them Irish?" The next question concerned migration; "say both parents are Irish and their child was born in Ireland and they moved away shortly after- does that make them Irish?" Other questions concerned language acquisition, knowledge or engagement with various Irish and non-Irish sports and questions of returning emigrants who settle but have borne children abroad. I attempted, in each instance, to enter into dialogue about the question and to parse out the individual components of what would allow us to consider someone to be Irish or not. She was able to cite a number of instances in which someone had thought themselves to be Irish even though others had resisted that interpretation.

Ultimately, and as our train pulled into the station, she confided in me that she had presumed that my work would serve as a litmus test for whether someone could rightly be considered 'properly Irish' or not and she wished me the best of luck with it.

Not all encounters though necessarily incur dejection or result in the desire for a litmus test; still, what might we make of instances in which a seamless passing occurs and in which a non-Irish person might 'pass' as a member of the Irish community? It is to this question I wish to turn in the section which follows:

Jackson (2008), in describing the difficulties faced by undocumented Sierra Leonian migrants in London describes a process of 'passing'. What is meant by passing is the seamlessness between self and other which allows for 'passing' to occur. Jackson's ethnography concerns migrants who affect a North-London approximation of the retort: "wha?" to their being accosted. The key to passing in this manner was to mimic the accent of the locals such that your presence was tacitly accepted and your belonging imagined. As observed previously in the instance of the dejected Australian, passing in the instance of people who imagine themselves to be Irish often result in their dismissal. This phenomenon is ascribed, in Slattery (2010) as a judgment which is somehow innate to Irish people and which begins at the local level and emanates outward:

> The practical approach if you find yourself in this position [if you should move to Ireland, ed.] is not to become Irish but to pretend to be Irish. We Irish will always be able to tell the difference even if you can't...

> [Plastic Paddies, ed.] think they are really Irish but it is practically impossible to fake it. (Slattery, 2010:38)

Slattery's account here is an attempt at a wry transmission of the state of affairs concerning the lack of seamlessness of Irish culture and its receptivity to Others. It is curious that Slattery's more programmatic account of Irishness in 2011 stands in contrast to an earlier examination of the role played both by the notion of simulation to ethnographic examination as well as to the relation that simulation has to the rise in procedures of authentication:

> Simulation is the postmodern mode of signification that produces an economy of signs through which we think ourselves in culture and through which we communicate. Obviously the meaning of simulations often escapes us at a conscious level, so there is a need to unpack their cultural values: this is the heuristic strategy... The idea of authenticity belongs to history at the level of history's relation to reality, but it belongs to postmodern experience in terms of authenticating procedures. (Slattery, 2003:146-147)

It is at that very point in the ethnographic process that the author has to resign himself to the fact that his efforts to discover a fully-fledged and authentic capitulation of Dublin, which he is doing for the benefit of some academics-cum-tourists whom he is showing around the area, is doomed to failure. He closes the section, from which the above quote is drawn, with the observation that "[D]ublin cannot be authentic in a naively realist way" (Ibid:147). Slattery's interjection, then, seems both to be that there exists something akin to a safety net which, a priori, allows people make a determination of the kind that you are *not* from Ireland while acknowledging that authenticity has faded into the middle distance but that authenticating procedures still loom large. That being said, I have never seen an informant, Catalin, as happy, than on the occasion on which he was mistaken for an Irish person the occasion on which this force of authentication was not as present as Slattery contends that it is.

Whereabouts in Donegal are you from? Misattribution and Pride

A friend, having arrived late to conversation who was, herself, completely fluent in the Irish language joined the table at which myself, Catalin and Emma were all sat. She introduced herself and where she was from to each of us and asked the same of us and we patiently heard from everyone present. Finally, she reached Catalin but having heard his accent her interrogative approached changed slightly. "Is ea. Agus carbh as I nDun na Gall thú?" ["I see, and whereabouts in Donegal are you from?"] Catalin glanced over at me almost immediately and a massive smile overtook his face. The woman who asked the question was immediately concerned that she had insulted him, but as she was trying to apologise Catalin interjected asking everyone what they would like to drink. He was ecstatic, not to have been mistaken, but rather to have passed, without having deceived anyone, as Irish temporarily and to have exceeded narrowly drawn, reductive lines of semblance which are often correlated to legitimacy.

Catalin had become excitable only when he overcame the reduction to inauthenticity, when he came to occupy a broader, seamless Irishness to which everyone was welcome. Catalin is not alone in attempts of this kind and other efforts, as mediated through the conveyance of language, assist in the negotiation of the all too sharply drawn contours of Irishness and representation.

Concluding remarks:

In closing then, this work has attempted to tease out the contextual specificities of how communities are imagined, transposed onto foreign contexts, felt to be under threat and critiqued and the manner in which this negation of belonging can become superseded. The vastness of the Irish diaspora worldwide and the lack of direct exposure that individuals have to the 'home' place become a battle ground in which imaginaries and counter-imagined rejections play out. The very idea of community, given the impossibility of representing itself to itself, gives rise to the understanding that it is an imagined construct. Delving further we see the troubled composition of imaginaries with respect to statements of an ancestral kind, and the twin desires to reiteratively reinstate the role played by the nation-state in the composition of belonging as well as instances in which the belonging is extended overseas.

The lenticular apparatus of the imaginary is a necessity to frame the diaspora, to determine claims of belonging and of sameness, but it can also be reappropriated as a kind of binary distinction-making tool which results in heartache and dejection. This has been contextualised against the backdrop of the Irish in Belgium and put into dialogue with those ethnographic vignettes which speak to the concern of belonging and how it might be imagined. In attempting to trace the manner in which imagined claims are received we arrive at the assertion that communities abroad are imagined in an altogether different way than communities which are conceived of as being more territorially bound and that diaspora communities need a special theoretical treatment, some movement in the direction of which I have attempted to suggest here.

Bibliography:

Adorno, Theodor. *The Jargon of Authenticity*. Transl. Tarnowski, K. & Will, F. London: Routledge, 2003.

Althusser , Louis. *Essays on Ideology*. London & New York: Verso Books, 1971.

Anderson, Beneditc. *Imagined Communities: Reflections on the Origin and Spread of Nationalism*. London: Verso, 1983.

Bauman, Zygmunt. . *Liquid Modernity*. Massachusetts: Polity Press, 2000.

Benjamin Walter. *Illuminations*, trans. by H. Zohn, ed. with intro. by Arendt, Hannah., NY: Pimlico, 1999[1969].

Boland, Eavan. "The Emigrant Irish" in *World: Poems on the Underground*. London: Underground Companies, 2012.

Boylorn, Robin. & Orbe, Mark. *Critical Ethnography: Intersecting identities in everyday life*. Left Coast Press: California, USA, 2014.

Bronwen, Walter. et al. *A Study of the Existing Sources of Information and Analysis about Irish Emigrants and Irish Communities Abroad*. Dublin: Task Force Research Study, Minister for Foreign Affairs, 2002.

Collins, Peter & Gallinat, Anselma.*The Ethnographic Self as Resource: Writing Memory and Experience into ethnography*. Berghahn: New York, USA, 2010.

Cronin, Michael. Minding Ourselves : A New Face for Irish Studies, *Field Day Publications, 4*, 174-185, 2008.

Cronin, Michael. & Adair, Daryl. *The wearing of the green. A history of St Patrick's Day*. London: Routledge, 2002.

Deleuze, Gilles. & Guattari, Felix. *Kafka: toward a Minor Literature*. Translated by D. Polan. Minnesota: University of Minnesota Press, 1986.

_____ *Thousand Plateaus*. Translated by Massumi, Brian. London: Continuum Press, 1988.

Hall, Stuart. Cultural identity and diaspora. In Rutherford, John (Ed.), *Identity: community, culture, difference*. London: Lawrence & Wishart. 222-237, 1990.

Ignatiev, Noel. *How the Irish Became White*. New York: Routledge, 1995.

Jackson, Michael. The shock of the New: On migrant imaginaries and critical transitions. *Ethnos*, 73(1). 57-72, 2002.

Jenkins, Roy. Imagined but not imaginary: Ethnicity and Nationalism in the modern world. In MacClancy, J. (Eds.) *Exotic No More: Anthropology on the Front lines*. Chicago: University of Chicago Press. 114-128, 2002.

Leite, Naomi. Travels to an Ancestral Past: On Diasporic Tourism, Embodied Memory, and Identity. *Antropologicas*, 9: 273–302, 2005.

Mauss, Marcel. Techniques of the Body. Economy and Society, Vol 2(1). 70-88, 1973.

Mclean, Stuart. *The Event and its Terrors: Ireland, Famine, Modernity*. Stanford, CA: Stanford University Press, 2004.

Meillassoux, Quentin. *After Finitude: An Essay on the Necessity of Contingency*. New York: Continuum, 2008.

Niezen, Ronald. *The Origins of Indigenism: Human Rights and the Politics of Identity*. Berkeley: University of California Press, 2003.

Nora, Pierre. Between Memory and History: Les Lieux de Memoire. *Representations*, 26, 7-24, 1989.

Nora, P. (Eds.). *Realms of Memory: Rethinking the French Past.* New York: Columbia University Press, 1996.

O' Dubhghaill, Sean. "It's fake – I mean it sounds the same, but it's fake": Plasticity, simulation and passing through the Irish Language in Belgium. *Irish Journal of Anthropology*, 17(1), 46-51, 2014.

Quinn, Ellen Moore. Not Quite Dyed in the Wool: Weaving Selfhood in Ireland. *Journal of the Society for the Anthropology of Europe*, 1(2), 28-42, 2001

Rains, Stephanie. 'Roots and Routes: Irish-American Interest in Genealogy, 1945-2000'. In: Negra, Diane (eds.) *The Irish In Us: Irishness, Performativity, and Popular Culture*, Duke University Press: Durham, NC, 2006.

Salazar, Noel, & Graburn, Nelson. (Eds.) *Tourism imaginaries: Anthropological approaches.* Oxford: Berghahn, 2014.

Slattery, David. Fear and loathing in Lost ages: journey through postmodern Dublin in Coulter, C. & Coleman, S. (Eds.) *The End of Irish History? Critical Reflections on the Celtic Tiger.* Manchester: Manchester University Press. 139-154, 2003.

_____ *How to be Irish: Uncovering the Curiosities of Irish Behaviour.* Dublin: Orpen Press, 2011.

Taylor, Charles. *Modern Social Imaginaries.* North Carolina: Duke University Press, 2004.

Williams, Raymond. *Keywords: A vocabulary of culture and society.* New York: Oxford University Press, 1985.

www.ingramcontent.com/pod-product-compliance
Lightning Source LLC
Chambersburg PA
CBHW061750020426
42331CB00006B/1414